GREEN LONDON

GREEN LONDON

Fourteen Walks Exploring London's Green Spaces and Pathways

Written & illustrated by
DAVID FATHERS

CONWAY

LONDON · OXFORD · NEW YORK · NEW DELHI · SYDNEY

CONTENTS

FOREWORD

I thought I knew London, but who *really* knows London? It is the Great Wen, the Great Smoke, Blighty, no hold on, Blighty refers to the whole of England. The point is that London is a whopper. So huge, so sprawling, so ancient, so much to see, so much to do. And so wonderful. Oh yes it is. Always exciting, stimulating, innovative. Shame about the traffic.

I moved to London in the Swinging Sixties and like to think that over the last 60 years, I have visited most parts of the city, but that is a bit of a fib. How could any normal human with only two legs and lungs manage it all? There are probably nine-tenths of it I have still not visited. But what I do know, I love it dearly. If you tire of London, as someone nearly said, you might as well be dead.

London's greatest glory is its greenery: all those parks, gardens and open spaces. No other city in the world has been so blessed. I like to think I have walked all the major London parks, and written about them, as many have walked and written about them before. But I am so jealous of David Fathers for his original format.

Instead of sticking to the usual park boundaries, limiting himself to the park railings, he has included in each of his 14 wonderful walks all the adjoining parks and green spaces: the titchy bits, the hidden bits, which locals may know and love but visitors can easily miss. He has worked out green routes, paths and ways in each area, to link the well-known parts together while taking in woods, canal paths and riversides. In a way, he has turned *all* London green. And along the way, he has drawn our attention to trees, statues, monuments and famous folks and moments in history.

I learned so much, even about areas and parks I thought I knew so well, Ally Pally, for example. I live not far from it. I also know Finsbury Park, as one of my daughters live near. But Abney Park Cemetery, you what, where is that? I'd never heard of it! But I am off in the morning to visit.

Most of all, I envy David's artistic skills. His maps are fab, his diagrams and illustrations incredibly helpful. Everything is so easy to follow and appreciate. And ever so useful. I can imagine some readers buying the book and just sitting, reading and ogling each spread, forgetting to get out there and walk. You know, moving the legs forward.

David's hand-crafted, beautiful, atmospheric, eerie, moody digital images enhance every page. They are works of art in themselves. In fact, the book itself is a work of art. Don't just use it, and learn from it, but admire and appreciate it. It should give joy to everyone who loves London, both locals and visitors.

Hunter Davies, 2024

*I walk here as much as I can, but I'm very busy.
It's absolutely beautiful here (even though it's in
the city). There are lilacs and hawthorns and
laburnums &c. blossoming in all the gardens,
and the chestnut trees are magnificent.*

Vincent Van Gogh

writing to his brother while living in
London, 30 April 1874.

INTRODUCTION

A verdant capital

Some years ago, shortly after my arrival in London, I was living in Muswell Hill. It was Saturday in late September and I was due to go out for dinner that evening with friends. However, I had left my cheque book and bank card (yes, it was that long ago) at my place of work in an area now known as Fitzrovia. The weather forecast was good for that day, so I considered walking the 11km into town.

I knew already there was a disused railway line nearby that was frequented by walkers and cyclists (this path would, a few years later, become the northern section of the Parkland Walk). So, after consulting my dog-eared A–Z, I plotted out a route that would involve walking on as few urban walkways as possible. My route, after the old railway line, involved crossing through Highgate Wood and village, onto Hampstead Heath, Primrose Hill, Regent's Park and then my final destination and the cheque book. Little did I know that London could be so traversed by using green paths only. This journey might have planted an idea in the back of my head but it would be another 40 years before the notion germinated and I would begin to assemble these routes together as an illustrated guidebook.

A battle for green space

There are so many places in Greater London that conjure up forms of leafy spaces, for example; Stroud Green, Shepherd's Bush, Cricklewood and Hither Green. These names hark back to a time hundreds of years ago, when these locations were open spaces away from the noisome confines of the capital. Beginning in the 18th century the capital expanded rapidly and began to devour huge chunks of woods, farms and ancient forests.

Fortunately, by a mixture of good luck, altruism and serious campaigning, some of the heaths and open spaces managed to survive. Many of the parks had been privately or royally owned and often walled off to keep the wildlife in and the commoners out.

By the 19th century, it had become apparent that big open spaces were essential for the benefit of all to escape the smoke and grime of ever-sprawling industrialised London. Victoria Park in the north-east of the capital and Battersea Park were formed as fine green open spaces and, similarly, several of the Royal Parks, including Hyde Park, gradually became accessible to all. Along the way in this guidebook I attempt to highlight some of the struggles to protect and preserve the capital's green spaces.

This process of improving London's green spaces and corridors has continued over the past 50 years. Invigorated by the arrival of the Olympic Games in 2012, the banks along the River Lea and the Lee Navigation have been transformed from a heavily industrialised environment into a very pleasant verdant walk from Tottenham down to London's brand-new Queen Elizabeth Olympic Park and beyond. In the River Wandle, brown trout have returned to the stream with some human assistance (although a recent increase in river pollution isn't helping). Several wetlands, adjacent to reservoirs around the outskirts of the capital, although once closed, are now accessible to walkers. Disused railways tracks that once led to the giant Victorian exhibition centres of Crystal and Alexandra Palace have now become fabulous green interconnecting corridors. And in the East End, a green walkway sits on top of a huge 19th-century sewer pipe.

The forest of London

There are about eight million trees in Greater London. That's almost one per head of the city's population. Furthermore, a definition by the United Nations Food and Agricultural Organization, a contiguous area with a minimum of 10 per cent tree canopy cover is a forest, thus making London a forest!

Over the past 12 years, while I've been researching material for this and my other London guidebooks, I've discovered just how truly verdant London is, with thousands of parks, over-grown cemeteries, towpaths and tree-lined walkways. It is an almost endless place to walk and discover.

Above: the Wetland Walk, Queen Elizabeth Park.

USING THIS BOOK

The walks featured in this guidebook cover a total of 132km (or 82 miles) and are broken down into 14 walks of distances varying from 2.8km to 13.7km. These are displayed just below the chapter title. Each route could easily be walked in a reverse sequence, if desired. The route is indicated with a red dotted line. Occasionally a path or street may be closed due to building or engineering works. In these circumstances, there are usually alternative routes signposted by the contractors.

Many of the woodland paths featured in this guidebook are not always signposted and navigation can be difficult at times. In this instance I would recommend, if possible, using the GPS features on a smartphone (e.g. Google Maps).

All nearby Underground, Overground and railway stations are clearly marked on the maps throughout the book.

Symbols

Opposite: the Albert Memorial and the Royal Albert Hall.

CENTRAL LONDON

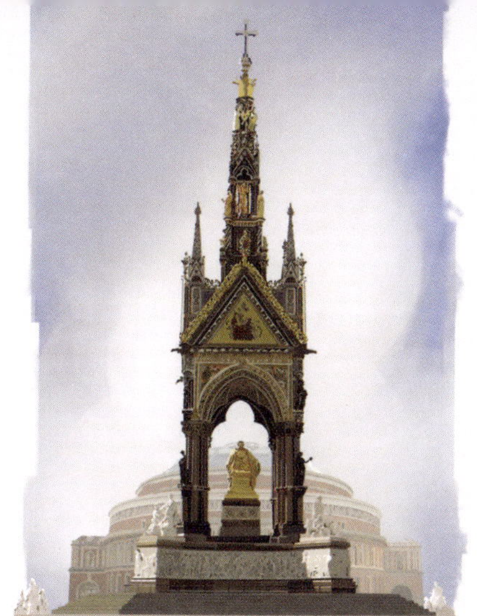

HYDE PARK & KENSINGTON GARDENS

HYDE PARK CORNER – ST JAMES'S PARK

These four Royal Parks form central London's largest piece of green space. They are home to numerous memorials to departed royalty, war heroes, Holocaust victims, animals and even a fictitous character.

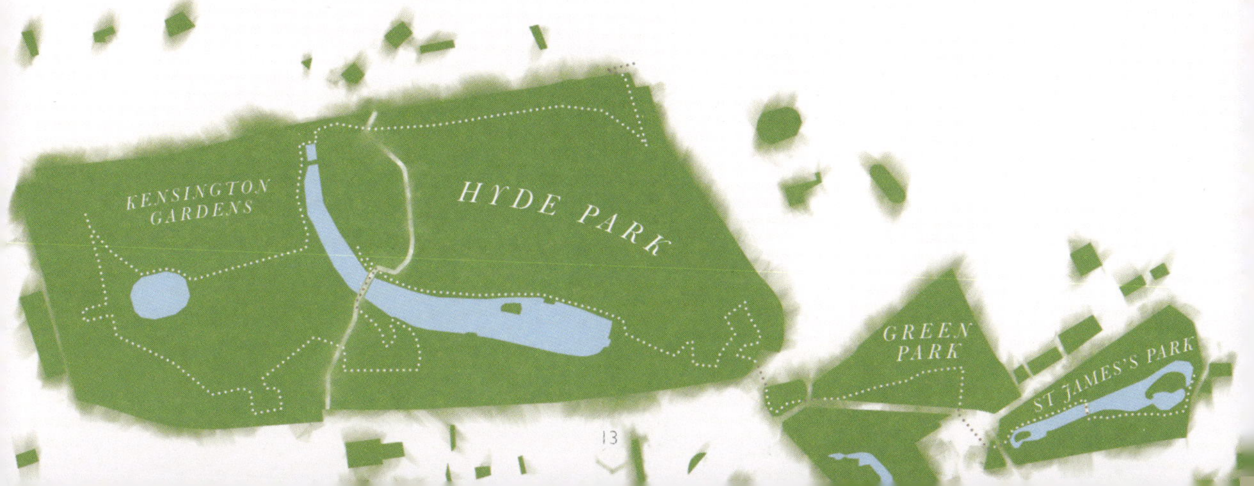

HYDE PARK & KENSINGTON GARDENS

Total walking distance 8.6km

These two Royal Parks combined make up the largest area of green space in Central London and are extremely popular with locals and tourists alike. Many come just to walk, exercise or take in the views. Five hundred years ago these grounds looked very different. The estate was then owned by the Abbot of Westminster, until Henry VIII acquired the land from the church and converted it into deer hunting grounds. It was only in 1851, the year that the Great Exhibition opened, that the general public were allowed access to the parks. Today, the parks are managed by a charity, The Royal Parks.

1 The Tyburn Tree Within the pedestrian island is a simple pavement plaque marked 'The Site of the Tyburn Tree'. This is believed to be the site where three elm trees once stood*, and beginning in the 12th century it became an established place of execution. The condemned were transported from Newgate prison or the Tower of London to this, then-remote location, west of the capital.

Over time execution days became big events with large crowds gathering.

The three trees were replaced in 1571 with a triangular wooden structure, large enough to execute 24 people at a time. Such was the popularity of these macabre occasions that the landowners constructed grandstands and charged an entrance fee.

In 1783, the government prohibited further executions at Tyburn as, following the Gordon Riots of 1780, they feared the gathering of such large crowds. Also, London was expanding westwards and occupants of the new houses of Marylebone and Mayfair didn't want such gruesome events occurring nearby.

** It is now believed that the Tyburn Tree actually stood some 200m away in the south-east corner of Connaught Square (1b).*

2 Marble Arch This ceremonial gateway, built of white Carrara marble and designed by John Nash in 1826, was originally located outside the front of Buckingham Palace. When the new palace façade was added to the eastern side, the arch, now being too close to the royal abode, was dismantled and rebuilt here in 1851, on this rather lonely spot within a busy traffic island.

3 Speaker's Corner A large crowd of 150,000 people gathered on this spot in 1855 to protest against Lord Robert Grosvenor's proposed Sunday Trading Act. The motion would ensure pubs, shops and public transport would not be allowed to trade on the

Sabbath. However, this was the only day most working people had free in the week. The Act would therefore not affect many wealthy folk. After one orator rose to speak, the police attempted to arrest him. He managed to escape but a riot then ensued. Karl Marx was in attendance that day and later wrote that this was 'the beginning of the English revolution'. The following day, Grosvenor withdrew the bill.

The site then soon became a popular destination for protestors and in 1866 the Reform League met here to demand votes for all men, regardless of status. In 1872, an Act of Parliament enshrined the right of free speech at Speaker's Corner so long as it wasn't seditious, blasphemous or liable to incite violence. Many famous orators have addressed rallies here including Vladimir Lenin, William Morris, Marcus Garvey, George Orwell and of course Marx. In the age of social media, Speaker's Corner now has less significance.

4 The Italian Gardens The levels of The Long Water and The Serpentine lakes were maintained by the River Westbourne. However, as the 18th century progressed and London expanded, the river became increasingly polluted with human and industrial waste. The lakes began to smell, so a set of filter ponds were created at the head of the lakes to clean the water before it entered The Long Water. This wasn't a total success and by 1850 the Westbourne was culverted around the lakes. The Serpentine and The Long Water were then fed water from a borehole and the filter beds were converted into ornamental ponds with a fountain and surrounding gardens. An Italianate pavilion (still standing) once housed the steam engine that powered the fountains.

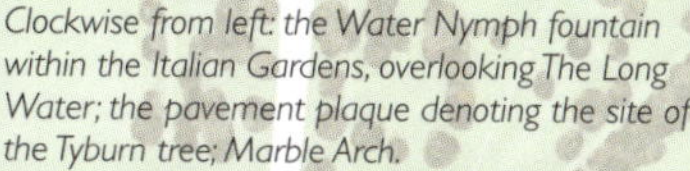

Clockwise from left: the Water Nymph fountain within the Italian Gardens, overlooking The Long Water; the pavement plaque denoting the site of the Tyburn tree; Marble Arch.

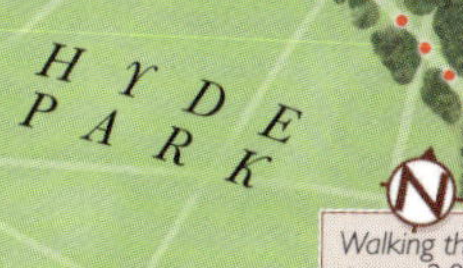

15

1 The Peter Pan statue

The author JM Barrie wrote the children's novel *Peter Pan or The Boy Who Wouldn't Grow Up* in 1904. Part of the story is set in Kensington Gardens and it was here that Barrie, in 1912, had the statue of Peter Pan erected. It appeared in the gardens overnight and without permission to give the impression that it had magically arrived. The 4.3m-tall statue was created by Sir George Frampton and features Peter Pan blowing a wind instrument, with mice, female figures and rabbits decorating the base.

2 The Round Pond

The pond was created in the 1730s as a focal point for the garden paths. Despite its name it is actually an octagonal pond, and is used by model boaters and ducks.

3 The Peter Pan 'Tombstones'

In the novel *Peter Pan*, author JM Barrie macabrely describes Peter collecting bodies of babies that had fallen out of their prams and died without the mothers noticing, and then burying them within the gardens. The gravestones are actually parish boundary markers and are inscribed W. St M. (Westminster St Margaret) and 13A P. P. (Parish of Paddington). In Barrie's creative mind these were the gravestones of Walter Stephen Matthews and Phoebe Phelps. The stones have eroded over the years.

4 The Elfin Oak

This sculpted ancient oak tree stump was created by Ivor Innes in 1930. It has been restored several times and is now caged to protect the tree and its decorations of fairies and animals.

5 Kensington Palace & Gardens

After ascending the throne in 1689, William III and his wife Mary bought a mansion and grounds from the Earl of Nottingham in the village of Kensington, to the west of London. They then set about redeveloping the property as a London palace, away from the damp and smoky air of Whitehall.

Access to the gardens was granted only to the well-heeled visitors whenever the Royal Court moved to Richmond. The gatekeepers ensured no servants, workers or soldiers could enter the grounds.

Almost every new monarch set about adding new features to the estate. Queen Anne, crowned in 1702 following the death of William III, commissioned Nicholas Hawksmoor to design the Orangery as an addition to the palace.

A huge water feature, The Long Water, was added in 1730, when the River Westbourne was dammed (page 20). The wife of George II, Queen Caroline, acquired 80ha of Hyde Park to expand the

Clockwise from above: a detail from the Elfin Oak; the Peter Pan statue; the Peter Pan 'Tombstones'; Kensington Palace with a statue of Queen Victoria, sculpted in 1893 by her fourth daughter, Princess Louise, Duchess of Argyle.

gardens and added the Round Pond. She even had a 46m-high observation mound created in 1733, complete with a rotating summerhouse on the peak. The hill was eventually taken down.

Dissatisfied with the Kensington royal abode, George III moved his court to St James's Palace. However, Queen Victoria, who was born in Kensington Palace in 1819, was said to have loved the place. It was here that she learned of the death of William IV, making her Queen. Within weeks she was residing in Buckingham Palace.

Following the sudden death of Diana, Princess of Wales, in 1997, huge amounts of floral tributes were placed by the palace gates, as this had been her place of residence for several years. Today, apartments within the palace are home to several members of the royal family including the Prince and Princess of Wales and their children, the Duke and Duchess of Gloucester, and Princess Michael of Kent. *A fee is charged for entry to the palace.*

1 The Albert Memorial This huge 53m-high structure of marble, bronze and mosaics is a monument to Queen Victoria's husband Prince Albert, who had suddenly died of typhoid in 1861, aged 42. Within weeks of his demise a competition was proposed to create a lasting memorial to the Queen's consort. The contest was won by the 'high priest' of Victorian Gothic Revival, the architect George Gilbert Scott. The final memorial, in the form of a canopy, featured details of the life and interests of the prince, and was finally revealed in 1872, although it would be another four years before his statue was added. The seated figure of Prince Albert holds a copy of the Great Exhibition catalogue.

2 Royal Albert Hall This concert hall, which opened in 1871, has become a much-loved venue for music performances, award ceremonies, film screenings, sporting events and the annual BBC Proms.

Prince Albert was very keen to use the profits made from the 1851 Great Exhibition to develop several museums and a music venue within the South Kensington district. The project to design and build the Royal Albert Hall stalled several times and it wasn't until 1865 that the final plans for an oval auditorium, designed by civil engineer Captain Francis Fowke, were approved.

Not long after the venue

Clockwise from above: a ring-necked parakeet, a common sight in Kensington Gardens; the Albert Memorial with the Royal Albert Hall behind; a Crystal Palace information pavement plaque.

opened it became apparent that the domed structure created an echo, which was unsuitable for musical or spoken performances. At the time it was said that it was 'the only place where a British composer could be sure of hearing his work twice'. The acoustic problem wasn't fully remedied until 1968.

The organ, with its 9,999 pipes, is the second largest in the UK. Starting in 1996, the venue, now a Grade I listed building, underwent a £40m programme of renovation that included a new porch on the south side.

3 Serpentine Galleries The Serpentine Galleries consist of two buildings: one to the south of the lake (shown here), within Kensington Gardens, and the other a five-minute walk away, to the north across the bridge. Both galleries have recently been rebranded 'Serpentine'.

The Serpentine South Gallery is a brick-built structure, constructed in 1934 as a tea pavilion for visitors to Hyde Park and Kensington Gardens. In 1970, the pavilion was converted into a gallery. Over the years the exhibition space has displayed works by many leading international artists including Jeff Koons, Anish Kapoor, Marina Abramović, Henry Moore and Damien Hirst. Each year since 2000, Serpentine has commissioned a renowned international architect to create a temporary pavilion in the grounds adjacent to the gallery. These have included Zaha Hadid (2000), Daniel Libeskind (2001), Herzog & de Meuron (2012) and Sou Fujimoto (2013).

The Serpentine North Gallery (page 21) was created out of a former early 19th-century gunpowder store and opened

to the public as a gallery in 2013. A ray-fish-shaped extension was designed by Zaha Hadid Architects. Both galleries are free to enter.

4 The Great Exhibition In 1851, the then largest exposition ever seen in the world took place on a 9ha site south of the Serpentine. The Great Exhibition was the brainchild of Prince Albert, who wanted to display the huge advances that Britain had made in science and technology.

A competition was held to design the exhibition hall and 230 entries were received. The glass edifice proposed by the gardener and engineer Sir Joseph Paxton was chosen. It would become the largest building in the world at the time. The Crystal Palace, as it was nicknamed, contained 14,000 exhibitors showing 100,000 exhibits, including railway engines, the Koh-i-Noor diamond, a precursor to the fax machine and flush toilets. Over the five months the exhibition was open it welcomed 6 million visitors.

When the Great Exhibition closed, the vast hall was dismantled and it was moved to a site in Sydenham, south London (page 113). The location would become known as Crystal Palace. Profits from the Great Exhibition of £186,500 (about £20m today) were used to establish the Victoria and Albert, Science and Natural History museums in South Kensington. The corners of the exhibition venue are marked with circular pavement information plaques (**4a**).

1 Diana Memorial Fountain This memorial, opened in July 2004 by Queen Elizabeth II, was designed by Kathryn Gustafson as a reflection of Diana's life – water cascades down in two separate channels and reunites in a calm pool at the bottom. The fountain had to be closed for improvements not long after it opened following several accidents involving visitors slipping on the stonework. Note, it is not a fountain in the classic sense of the word.

2 The Arch Inspired by a fragment of bone, artist Henry Moore created *The Arch*, a 6m-tall sculpture formed of Travertine marble. The piece is positioned so as to frame Kensington Palace 1km away to the west.

3 Hyde Park This is an extremely popular area of open green space within central London. The 142ha park offers horse riding, swimming, skating, rowing, walking and running. But it wasn't always so accessible. Until the early 16th century the land, complete with wild bulls, boar and deer, was known as the Manor of Hyde and owned by the Abbot of Westminster. In 1536, Henry VIII used the powers of dissolution to seize the estate from the church and convert the space into his own personal hunting ground.

During the Civil War the land was sold off by the Parliamentarians, but upon the Restoration in 1660, Charles II oversaw the return of the estate and promptly enclosed it within a brick wall to retain the deer and keep the commoners out. The gatekeepers would only allow certain well-heeled people access to the grounds.

When William III moved into Kensington Palace (page 16), located to the west of the park, he had a road constructed to enable

access through Hyde Park to Whitehall. This route would later be known as Rotten Row.

During the 18th century the park became a popular location for differences to be settled by duelling. It is reported that over 60 people died here in such contests. In the early part of the 19th century the walls were removed, new gates installed and the general public given greater access to the park. The greatest event to occur here was the 1851 Great Exhibition (page 19).

In the 20th century, the park was used to celebrate many royal anniversaries and weddings, including Elizabeth II's Silver and Diamond Jubilees. Since 2007, a Winter Wonderland event has taken place in the park each November and December. The festive gathering includes a Christmas market, ice skating, amusement rides, restaurants and bars.

Starting in 1968, the park featured many large music concerts. The Rolling Stones played here on 5 July 1969, shortly after the death of the band's guitarist, Brian Jones. Other major groups to play here include Pink Floyd and Queen. The benefit concert Live 8 event occurred here in 2005 and featured Paul McCartney, U2 and Madonna.

The park is often the gathering point of many demonstrations. A suffragette march entitled Women's Sunday and organised by Emmeline Pankhurst and the Women's Social and Political Union gathered 500,000 women and men to a rally in the park in 1908. The Stop the War (in Iraq) rally also gathered here in 2003.

4 The Serpentine The Serpentine and The Long Water were devised by Queen Caroline, wife of George II, in 1730.

They were created by damming the River Westbourne at the south-east end of the park and allowing the shallow valley of 5m-depth to flood. The Long Water was planned as a water feature within Kensington Gardens. Today, the lake is fed by three boreholes that extract water from the chalk strata. At the south-eastern end of the lake is an ornamental dam over which the water cascades into the Dell. Celebrations to mark the end of the Napoleonic Wars featured a re-enactment of the Battle of Trafalgar on the Serpentine.

Swimming was finally allowed in 1930, when a section of the southern lake was roped off. The politician and social reformer George Lansbury, then Commissioner of Works, introduced changing rooms for both sexes. The lido is usually open to swimmers during the summer months. However, every Christmas Day morning since 1864, the Serpentine Swimming Club has organised a 100-yard race here. In 1913, author JM Barrie donated the Peter Pan Cup for the event. On colder Christmas Days, the ice has to be broken before the race can occur. In 2012, the lake was the venue for the men's and women's triathlon and marathon swimming events. During the summer months a solar-powered boat plies between the north and south shores of the Serpentine.

Left: The Arch by Henry Moore. Right: Children at play in the Diana Memorial Fountain

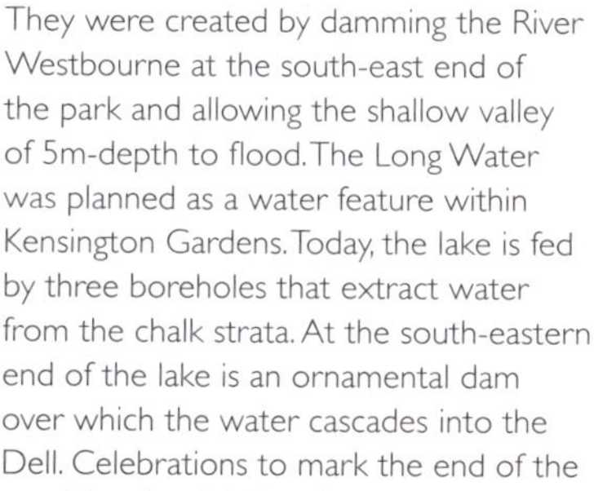

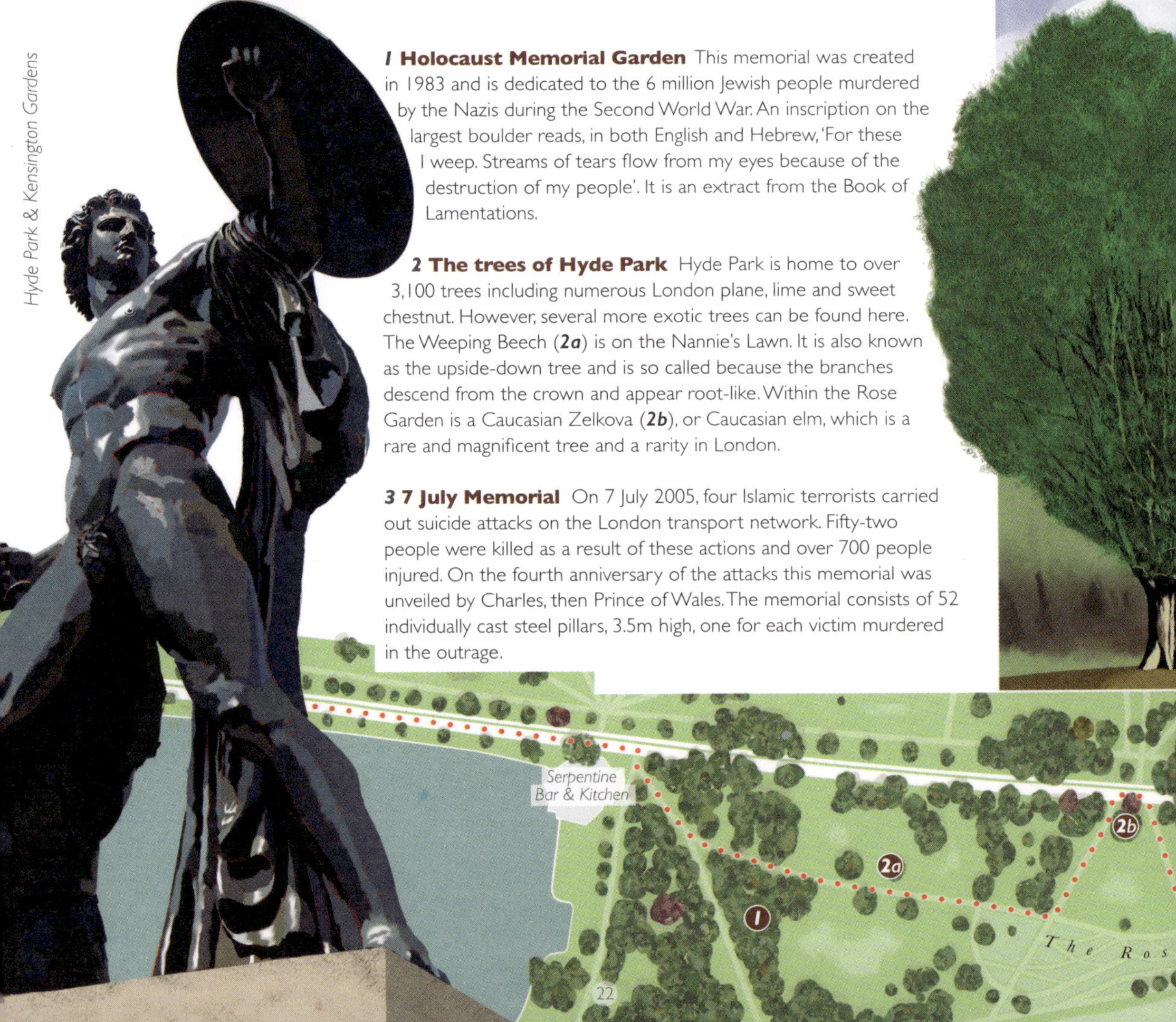

1 Holocaust Memorial Garden This memorial was created in 1983 and is dedicated to the 6 million Jewish people murdered by the Nazis during the Second World War. An inscription on the largest boulder reads, in both English and Hebrew, 'For these I weep. Streams of tears flow from my eyes because of the destruction of my people'. It is an extract from the Book of Lamentations.

2 The trees of Hyde Park Hyde Park is home to over 3,100 trees including numerous London plane, lime and sweet chestnut. However, several more exotic trees can be found here. The Weeping Beech (**2a**) is on the Nannie's Lawn. It is also known as the upside-down tree and is so called because the branches descend from the crown and appear root-like. Within the Rose Garden is a Caucasian Zelkova (**2b**), or Caucasian elm, which is a rare and magnificent tree and a rarity in London.

3 7 July Memorial On 7 July 2005, four Islamic terrorists carried out suicide attacks on the London transport network. Fifty-two people were killed as a result of these actions and over 700 people injured. On the fourth anniversary of the attacks this memorial was unveiled by Charles, then Prince of Wales. The memorial consists of 52 individually cast steel pillars, 3.5m high, one for each victim murdered in the outrage.

4 The Wellington Monument In 1822, a 5.5m-tall bronze statue of Achilles was erected here as a tribute to the Duke of Wellington, a leading military figure during the Napoleonic Wars and later prime minister. Money for the statue was raised by women of Britain, as mark of patriotism, and it was possibly the first almost naked statue to be publicly displayed in the country since Roman times. It was not modelled upon the duke himself but an ancient Roman statue of a horse trainer. The bronze for the sculpture came from French cannons captured during the Napoleonic Wars. The all-male committee organised to commission the statue instructed the sculptor to place a discrete fig-leaf over the statue's penis.

5 Apsley House From the rear windows of Apsley House, the Duke of Wellington must have been able to view the huge statue dedicated to himself. The home's official address was 'Number One, London', as it was the first house to be seen after passing the Knightsbridge tollgate. It was designed by Robert Adam for Henry Bathhurst, Lord Apsley, and completed in 1778, and was later acquired by the Duke of Wellington in 1817 as his London abode. By 1830, the duke had the red brick-built house clad with Bath stone. Following riots in the same year, in which the house was attacked, the duke had iron shutters placed over the windows, likely earning him his nickname of the 'Iron Duke'. During the 19th century, Piccadilly was lined with similar fine and impressive houses. Apsley House is one of the few survivors and is now a gallery and museum.

Hyde Park & Kensington Gardens

Clockwise from above: a detail from the 7 July Memorial; the Holocaust Memorial Garden; the Wellingtom Memorial; a Caucasian Zelkova (or Caucasian elm) in Hyde Park.

HYDE PARK CORNER – ST JAMES'S PARK

Total walking distance 2.8km

Although nowhere as big or busy as the neighbouring Royal Parks, Green Park and St James's Park offer a more relaxed environment. They are very popular in the spring and summer with workers seeking a tranquil lunch away from their desks. Numerous war memorials to those killed in two world wars line the route of this walk, while linking the two parks is the home of the British monarch, Buckingham Palace.

War memorials Within the space of 600m there are seven war memorials dedicated to the men and women who lost their lives in two world wars. Four are within Hyde Park Corner and the remaining three are located in Green Park.

		Dedicated
A	Royal Artillery Memorial	1925
B	Australian War Memorial	2006
C	Machine Gun Corps Memorial	1925
D	New Zealand War Memorial	2003
E	Commonwealth Memorial Gates	2002
F	RAF Bomber Command Memorial	2012
G	Canada Memorial	1994

1 Wellington Arch This arch was commissioned by George IV to commemorate British victories in the Napoleonic War (along with Marble Arch, page 14). The triumphal gateway, initially named 'Green Park Arch', was designed by Decimus Burton and was to be topped out with a four-horse chariot. The arch was completed in 1830.

A decade later, a campaign to immortalise heroes of the Napoleonic Wars led to a statue of Admiral Lord Nelson being placed upon a column in Trafalgar Square, and in 1846, an oversized 8.5m-tall statue of the Duke of Wellington on horseback was placed upon the Green Park Arch. It was then renamed Wellington Arch. The statue caused much controversy and debate. The government insisted that it be removed but the Duke threatened to resign all his posts. Reluctantly, the government backed down and the statue remained. By the late 1870s, the area became renowned for traffic jams and a new road traffic plan was proposed that involved moving the arch a short distance towards Constitution Hill. Work began in 1883 to dismantle

and relocate the arch and also remove the statue of Wellington (he had died over 30 years earlier). The northern section of the arch was converted into a police station, the smallest of its type in the capital.

In 1912, private funds finally enabled the bronze four-horse chariot to be commissioned and placed upon the Wellington Arch. Today, the arch is a small museum, isolated within a major traffic roundabout and accessible by pedestrian subways and crossings. It is possible to climb to the top of the arch.

2 Green Park Unlike its neighbours, Hyde Park and Kensington Gardens, Green Park has no landmark buildings of any description. The 20ha, bountiful with trees such as black poplar, lime and London plane, is a green corridor between Hyde Park and St James's Park.

In the 1660s, on the instruction of Charles II, part of the park became enclosed with a brick wall to retain the deer for hunting purposes. There is a mythical story regarding Catherine, the wife of Charles II. She once spotted him in the park, picking flowers for his mistress, so she ordered all the plants to be uprooted, meaning no flowers ever grew here and only the grass remained. However, it wasn't named Green Park until 1746.

The park slopes gently down towards Buckingham Palace and the slight valley indicates where the River Tyburn once ran. In the 18th century, the Chelsea Waterworks Company exploited the river to create a reservoir at the north end of the park to supply the local area with water. In the late 1830s, as the stream became more polluted, it was culverted beneath the park.

Green Park was used regularly for military training and manoeuvres. Following a successful outcome of the War of the Austrian Succession in 1748, firework celebrations were planned to be held in the park. George Frideric

Handel was commissioned to write a festive piece for the event (Music for the Royal Fireworks). However, things went horribly wrong. A Temple of Peace, a structure built for the celebrations, caught fire as the spectacle began, causing many fireworks to ignite prematurely. George II and his entourage had to move quickly to avoid harm, although at least one person was killed.

Green Park fell into disrepair following the death of George IV and plans to revive the park did not occur until Victoria took the throne. The reservoir was finally drained and filled in. Today, Green Park is a quiet oasis for office workers and visitors, away from the busy urban thoroughfares of Piccadilly and Hyde Park Corner.

Above: the Royal Artillery Memorial in Hyde Park Corner.
Right: Green Park sunbathers relaxing in deckchairs.

Walking these pages 1.3km

1 Buckingham Palace

The Buckingham Palace we see today is very different from the 18th-century townhouse owned by the Duke of Buckingham. In 1762, George III purchased the house from the duke as a London residence for his wife Charlotte, and renamed it the Queen's House. In 1820, when George IV ascended the throne, he set about expanding the house into a palace and commissioned architect John Nash to execute the royal commission.

William IV, George's brother, disliked the palace and never moved in. Instead, when he became king in 1830, he chose to remain in Clarence House. By then, the work was incomplete and the building was riddled with malfunctioning windows and bell pulls that never worked. Nash was dismissed and the architect Edward Blore was recruited to finish the project. Queen Victoria moved in almost as soon as she became queen in 1837 and subsequent monarchs have resided here ever since.

Blore later added the east-facing façade we see today, while the Marble Arch (page 14), which stood outside Buckingham Palace, was removed to its current site. He also created the famous balcony that was first used by Victoria in 1851. The palace contains around 600 rooms and has 18ha of private gardens. The Changing of the Guard can be witnessed outside the palace most days at 11am.

2 Victoria Memorial

In 1911, ten years after the death of Victoria, a vast commemorative statue was unveiled by her son, George V, just outside the gates of Buckingham Palace and sits within a memorial garden. Funds for the project were raised across the British Empire. The 25m-tall memorial of white Carrara marble features a seated Victoria, topped off with golden-winged Victory. Created by the sculptor Sir Thomas Brock, the statue celebrates Victoria's life and the empire she once ruled.

3 St James's Park

This was the first Royal Park to be created and is arguably one of the finest. The grounds were originally marshland, and the site of a women's leprosy hospital, named St James.

In the 1530s, Henry VIII bought the estate, had the land drained, the hospice demolished and a hunting lodge constructed in its place. James I later chose to clear many of the trees and had the grounds redesigned to include a menagerie and an aviary. Aptly, a road along the southern edge of the park became known as Birdcage Walk.

Upon gaining the throne, Charles II had the park restored, as it had suffered great damage during the Civil War. The ponds were converted into a 850m canal and the park became a popular spot for of the Battle of the Nile on the canal.

A gas-lit pagoda was constructed over the water with plans for a huge fireworks display. However, during the display, the structure ignited and collapsed into the canal, killing two men.

George IV had his favourite architect John Nash restyle St James's Park by removing the formal French designs by adding curved paths and a more natural-shaped lake. He also introduced London plane and black mulberry trees into the grounds.

The park's location today, surrounded by Buckingham Palace, St James's Palace and Westminster, make it a fine destination for visitors and office workers taking a lunchtime stroll. There are fabulous views to be seen from the Blue Bridge.

walking. However, it also gained a reputation for being the scene of licentious activities and, in 1822, it was illuminated with gaslight, making the footpaths safer to walk after dark.

To mark the victory over Napoleon, the Prince Regent invited heads of the victorious states to St James's Park in 1814 for a celebration with a re-enactment

4 Duck Island Cottage This quaint, multi-gabled cottage by the lake was built for the Ornithological Society in 1841. It is now the offices of the charity London Parks and Gardens.

Far left: the Victoria Memorial and Buckingham Palace. Left: view of Whitehall and the London Eye from the Blue Bridge; a pelican from St James's Park Lake (pelicans were sent as a gift from the Russian ambassador during the reign of James I).

Opposite: the panoramic view of Regent's Park and London beyond from Primrose Hill.

NORTH LONDON

HAMPSTEAD HEATH

PRIMROSE HILL – REGENT'S PARK

This is a walk across some of north London's finest heath and parkland. Spectacular views of the capital are never too far away.

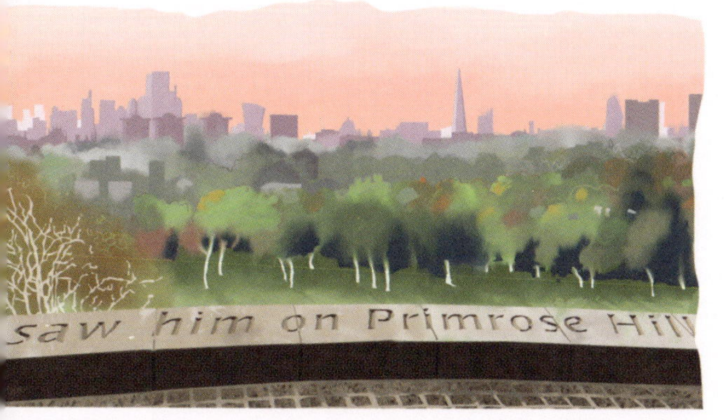

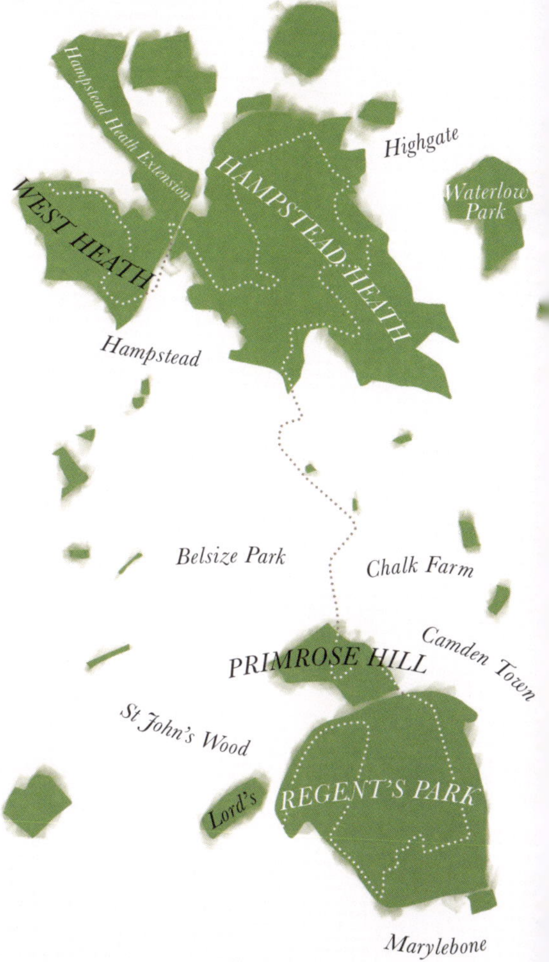

HAMPSTEAD HEATH

Total walking distance 9.3km

Today, Hampstead Heath is a place a lot of Londoners and visitors take for granted. It feels like it has been here and accessible forever. However, 150 years ago, this was certainly not the case, as most of the Heath was privately owned. As the population of Victorian London began to rapidly grow, a battle began between landowners who wanted to build on this green space and those who wanted to take the land into public ownership. This walk explores numerous parts of the Heath and reveals the struggles to make it into a free and open space for everyone.

1 Golders Hill Park In 1898, the grounds of Golders Hill Park and the house fell into public ownership. Today, the park is run by the City of London Corporation (which also manages Hampstead Heath). The park is a combination of flowers beds, grassed areas and trees. It features an enclosed fallow deer park and a free zoo that includes ring-tailed lemurs, wallabies, sacred ibises and Eurasian eagle owls. There is also a walled garden that was once part of the estate house. Unlike Hampstead Heath, this park is gated and is locked between the hours of sunset and sunrise.

2 The former Golders Hill House Close to the car park by the main gate is a flat area of grass overlooking the café and the parkland beyond. This was the location of Golders Hill House. When the owner of the house, Sir Thomas Spencer Wells, died in 1897, the house and grounds were put up for sale by auction and bought by Thomas Barratt, the chairman of the soap manufacturer A&F Pears. A year later he handed over his purchase to the London County Council for use by the public. In 1941, during the Second World War, Golders Hill House was destroyed by a parachute mine and never rebuilt.

3 Two Gibbet Elms On Inverforth Close, just off North End Way, once stood a pair of trees called Two Gibbet Elms. This was the site where, in 1674, the body of the executed highwayman and murderer Francis Jackson was left in a gibbet (a cage) for at least 17 years, as a grim warning to other would-be lawbreakers.

4 The Hill Garden and Pergola

This Italianate structure is a true hidden gem in north London. At the beginning of the 20th century Lord Leverhulme bought a large townhouse, then known as The Hill, on North End Way (today the house is known as Inverforth House). Leverhulme was an industrialist and philanthropist, who made a fortune selling Sunlight soap. In 1906, wishing to expand his garden to the south and west, he commissioned Thomas Mawson to design an outdoor, shaded

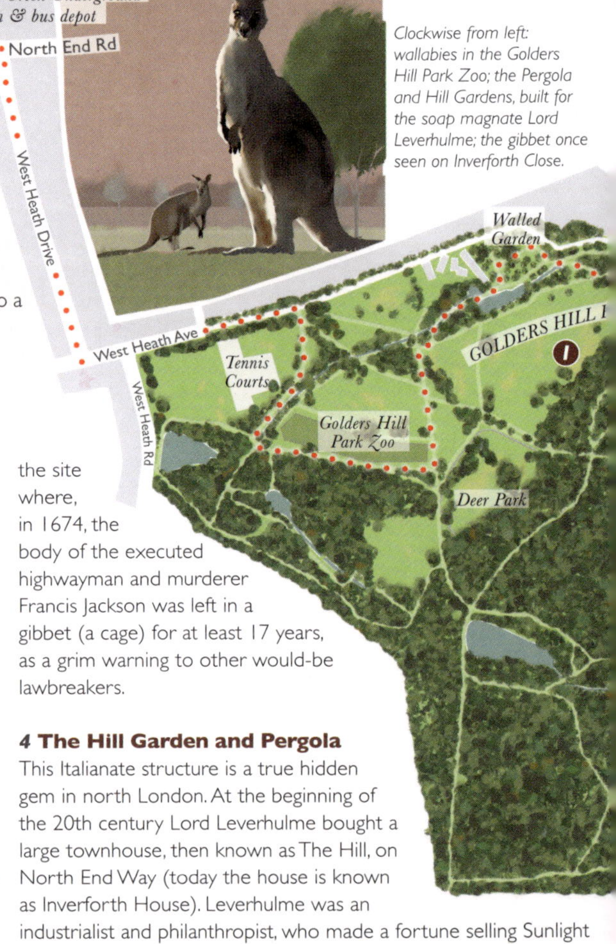

Clockwise from left: wallabies in the Golders Hill Park Zoo; the Pergola and Hill Gardens, built for the soap magnate Lord Leverhulme; the gibbet once seen on Inverforth Close.

terrace walkway or pergola that pushed out into the surrounding landscape. Mawson wanted it to be built on the same level as the house, but the garden sloped quickly away into West Heath. At this time a new underground tunnel was being constructed at Golders Green (it would later become a station on the Edgware branch of the Northern line), so some of the spoil from the tunnelling operation was moved to Inverforth House to level the garden. The pergola became an ideal setting for Edwardian garden parties, with views over West Heath and Harrow in the distance. Following the First World War the pergola was extended further to a length of 244m and completed in 1925, the same year in which Leverhulme died. The gardens and pergola, which are free to visit, are now managed by the City of London Corporation, although Inverforth House has been converted into a set of private residences.

5 West Heath This small, quiet section of sloping land, with distant views of Windsor and Heathrow Airport, is known as West Heath. It was painted by John Constable several times while he lived in Hampstead. The River Westbourne rises on the lower part of the slope, though it is now subterranean until it reaches the Thames in Chelsea. On Branch Hill, at the bottom of the slope, is a pair of four-storey Edwardian semi-detached houses. It was here, at The Chestnuts (**5a**), that the American singer and actor Paul Robeson lived from 1929 to 1930 (a plaque marks the house).

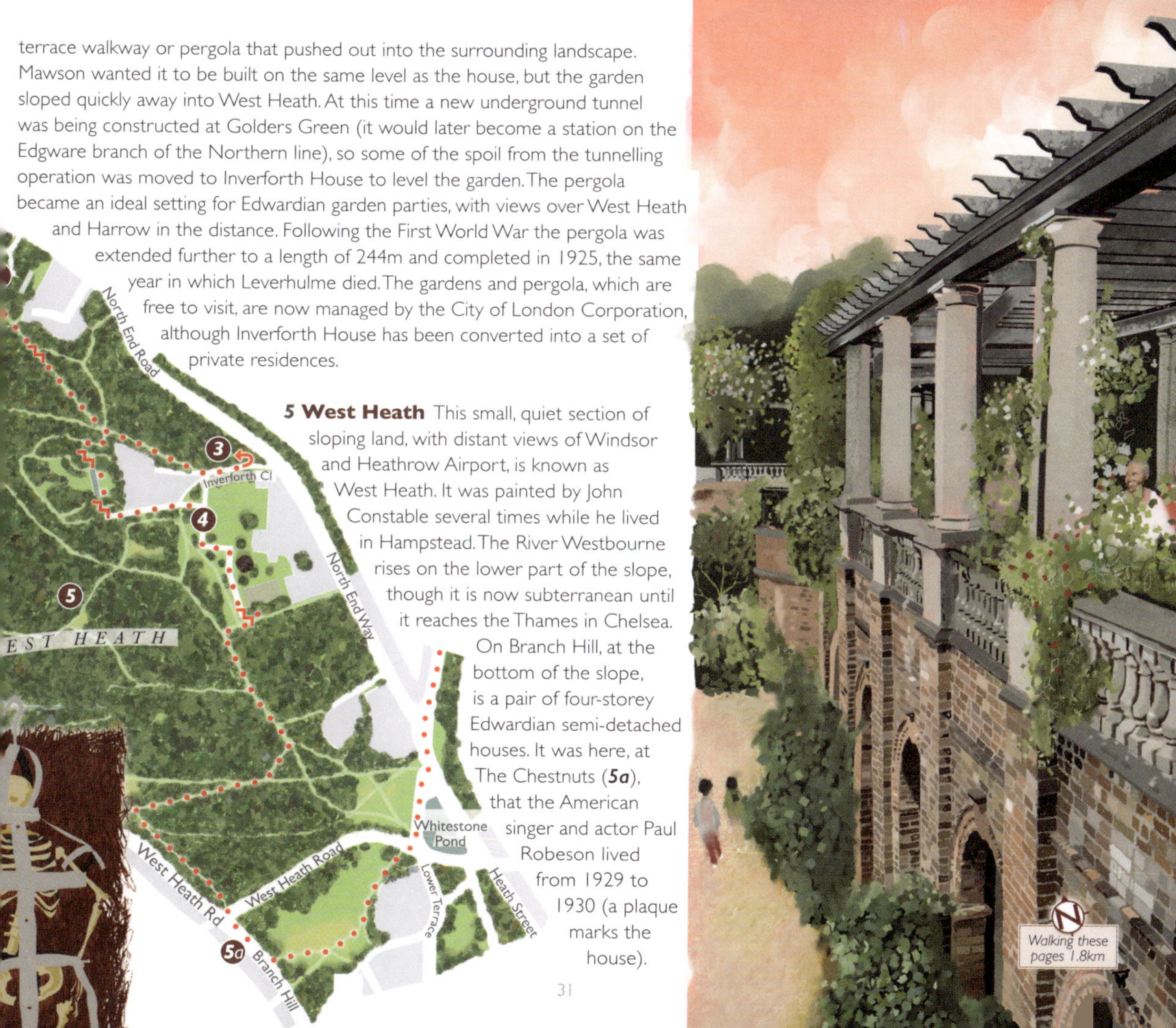

1 Whitestone Pond At 135m above sea level this is one of the highest points in north London. Once known as Horse Pond, it was originally created for horses towing wagons to be driven into the water in order to refresh themselves having just ascended one of the hills. The name Whitestone is taken from the white marker stone tucked away in the hedgerow between West Heath Road and Hampstead Grove. The pond is now artificially fed.

2 Jack Straw's Castle This building, now comprising of business and private residences, was once a public house built in the 18th century and overlooking the Heath. It was named after Jack Straw, one of the leaders in the 1381 Peasants' Revolt. It is possible that he stayed in a building on this site. The pub was destroyed by aerial bombing in 1941 and was later rebuilt.

3 Sandy Heath Sandy Heath appears more rugged than the neighbouring areas of open space. This high ridge is topped with Bagshot sand sitting upon a layer of clay. During the 19th-century building boom in the capital, sand was a vital commodity and therefore heavily extracted from this section of the Heath. Most of the ponds here are as a consequence of the sand being removed. Once the process of extraction had ceased, trees began to reclaim the terrain.

From left to right: Whitestone Pond and the flagpole; a human-made pond within Sandy Heath; a map showing the full extent of Hampstead Heath.

4 Hampstead Heath At 324ha, Hampstead Heath is London's largest piece of open space north of the Thames, and it attracts 8 million walkers, runners, swimmers and cyclists each year. It is famous for its wild swimming in the mixed and single-sex ponds and for its commanding views over the capital.

However, the Heath wasn't always so accessible or popular. A thousand years ago this area was a mixture of private estates and common land for grazing cattle, collecting wood and extracting sand. The name 'Hampstede' (a Saxon name meaning 'home stead') appeared in the Domesday Book in 1086.

The process of 'creating' Hampstead Heath began in 1871, when the Metropolitan Board of Works acquired 90ha of land, following the death of Sir Thomas Maryon Wilson (page 34). Incrementally, the Heath has grown as more sections of land were either bought or bequeathed. Its status now as open space is preserved by an Act of Parliament and it is designated a Site of Metropolitan Importance for Nature Conservation.

Hampstead Heath sits on layers of Bagshot Sand, Claygate Beds and London Clay. As rainwater filters through the sand and reaches the impermeable clay, it springs out to form small watercourses. These accumulate on the Heath to create three rivers, the Fleet, Westbourne and Brent, which descend into the Thames. The Fleet was dammed in places to create reservoirs to supply 18th-century London with potable water. Today, the Heath has around 20 ponds.

Since 1989, Hampstead Heath has been run by the City of London Corporation. It takes a staff of 130 people to manage the grasslands, trees, ponds and buildings, plus, a 12-strong constabulary to maintain order. The Heath, unlike Regent's Park, is kept in a natural state and has only a few small, managed ornamental gardens.

Trees of the Heath

Unsurprisingly, there is a large variety of trees to be found upon Hampstead Heath, including lime, oak and beech, and at least 800 trees, some of which are oaks, are well over 500 years old (thus giving them 'ancient' status). Many of these oaks defined the boundaries that once divided the Heath into private estates. These trees would have supplied a good harvest of acorns, an essential feed for pigs belonging to local farmers. Other trees such as hazel, hornbeam, field maple and alder are still a common sight. These were traditionally coppiced, and the wood used for fences, baskets and building material.

From the 17th century, several species of tree, including Swamp cypress and London plane, were imported and planted on the private estates of the Heath. The latter, despite its name, is not a native tree but was introduced from Spain or France in the 17th century and has gone on to survive well in the capital.

Walking these pages 1.4km

1 The Vale of Health

The scene here in the 18th century was very different to what we see today. The pond was a bog and the surrounding area, then known as Hatchett's Bottom, was infamous for the production of leather and varnish. The stench from works would have wafted across the Heath. In 1777, the Hampstead Water Company drained the bog to create a reservoir for the supply of clean drinking water.

Some 20 years later, the area was renamed (or rebranded) the Vale of Health. With the noisome factories banished and easy access to the Heath, it became a desirable place to live. In 1815, attracted by the seclusion, the radical Leigh Hunt came to live at Vale Lodge. He would often invite the poets John Keats and Percy Shelley to stay with him. One hundred years later, the novelist DH Lawrence and his wife Frieda lived at 1 Byron Villas in the Vale of Health. Other renowned residents included the painter Stanley Spencer, the publishers Alfred and Harold Harmsworth, and the Bengali poet and Nobel Prize winner Rabindranath Tagore.

2 Sir Thomas Maryon Wilson

The appearance of parts of the Heath can be attributed to Sir Thomas Maryon Wilson. Maryon Wilson was Lord of the Manor of Hampstead and owned a sizable piece of the Heath, though never lived there. He saw the chance to make a profit

by planning to build much-needed fine homes for the wealthy on his estate. In 1829, he requested permission to construct 28 houses, each with a sizeable garden. Parliament rejected this application and over the next 40 years he submitted a further 14 bills before Parliament, with the same intention. All of them were voted out.

Regardless, Maryon Wilson had a sizeable brick viaduct constructed over a pond for potential owners to drive their horses and carriages to their new abodes. Unused for its intended purpose, it quickly became known as Wilson's Folly. It is still in place today, though is now known as Viaduct Bridge.

Maryon Wilson continued to landscape the potential residential estates with hundreds of trees despite the lack of planning consent. It seemed almost like an act of revenge to 'spoil' the heath-scape with trees. Many of these trees are still present today. He also permitted brick makers to extract Claygate Clay for the production of the renowned yellow London bricks, on the site of what is now football fields on Viaduct Road.

The battle between those wishing to preserve the Heath and Maryon Wilson only came to an end when he died in 1869. Two years later his brother sold the land to the Metropolitan Board of Works for £45,000.

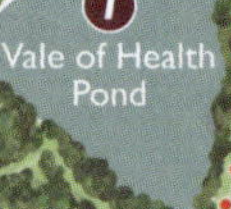

3 The Hollow Tree

This very unusual beech tree has had its base hollowed out over the years by the actions of fungi and bacteria. It was badly damaged during the 1987 storm, when part of the upper trunk broke off. Despite all this, the tree has survived. It has been claimed that up to 15 people managed to get inside the tree at one time. Fortunately, this activity is no longer encouraged and the tree is roped off.

4 Kenwood House

There has been a house on this site since the early 17th century. Between 1764 and 1779, the new owner William Murray, the soon-to-be 1st Earl of Mansfield, commissioned the architects Robert and James Adam to remodel the house in a neoclassical style. This is largely the building that we see today. The 2nd Earl added a dairy farm to the estate (a dairy out-building still stands to the west of the main house). While it provided produce for the family table, and it was profitable, it was considered fashionable among the aristocratic classes to have a vista of grazing cattle.

In 1772, as Lord Chief Justice, Mansfield presided over the case of James Somerset, an enslaved person living in England. His enslaver had planned to ship him to the Caribbean and there sell him. Supporters of Somerset took the matter to court. Mansfield eventually ruled that enslaved people could not be shipped out of the country against their will.

Kenwood House remained in the Mansfield family for over 250 years. However, in 1914, the 6th Earl attempted to sell the house for development, though was not successful. Finally, in 1925, Edward Cecil Guinness, 1st Earl of Iveagh, purchased the land and house. He filled the gallery with numerous pieces from his art collection, including works by Van Dyke, Rembrandt and Reynolds. Then, two years later, upon his death, he willed the house and contents to the nation.

The estate fell under the management of the Iveagh Bequest Trust, which ensured that the public were given free access to the grounds and house. Today, the 45ha estate of Kenwood House is managed by English Heritage and the grounds, demarcated by metal railings, are only open during daylight hours. The managed gardens contain many lime, Caucasian elm and London plane trees. There are also sculptures by Barbara Hepworth and Henry Moore on the lawns.

Clockwise from top left: The Viaduct Bridge over Viaduct Pond; the Hollow Beech tree and the rear (and probably more famous view) of Kenwood House overlooking the Wood; Thousand Pound Pond and London beyond.

Walking these pages 2.2km

1 Goodison Fountain This water fountain is named after Henry Goodison, founder of the Kenwood Preservation Society. The orange stains around its base are indicative of the iron-rich chalybeate water that flows out of the Heath.

2 Highgate Ponds At first glance these ponds, with overhanging trees and rushes, look very natural but they are, in fact, human-made.

As early as 1544, Henry VIII's Parliament was looking for new water supplies as existing ones were no longer adequate. Around the late 17th century, the Highgate Brook (one of the River Fleet tributaries) was dammed in several places by the Hampstead Water Company. The HWC leased the springs to create a series of reservoirs to supply potable water to the people of Kentish and Camden Towns. The water was carried via a set of hollowed-out elm boughs. This supply continued until the early 19th century by which time the water was deemed unsafe to consume.

Throughout the Victorian era swimming became increasingly popular as an activity. Indoor swimming pools were built across London and casual swimmers were taking the plunge in the Hampstead Heath Ponds.

Pressure grew for facilities such as changing rooms and an attendant to keep a safe eye on the swimmers. Eventually, in 1893, a men's bathing pond was opened. It would take another 33 years before a women's bathing pond was created.

3 Hampstead Heath Tumulus It was believed that Queen Boudica was buried beneath this tumulus following her defeat by the Romans in AD 60. It has also been suggested that the leader of the Trinobantes tribe may have been laid to rest here. Excavations have unearthed nothing to substantiate these claims.

4 Parliament Hill On a clear day it is worth a trip up the 98m summit to take in the views of London. Despite the presence of City skyscrapers, St Paul's Cathedral can still be seen in the distance. There are several theories behind the mound's name. It may have been used by the parliamentary army during the Civil War, or that it was to be the gathering point for members of the 1605 Gunpowder Plot to watch Parliament explode. However, Guy Fawkes was captured before the fuse was lit, and upon hearing this news the conspirators fled to Staffordshire. By the mid-18th century, the mound was known as Brock Hill. Kite flying has since become a popular activitity, meaning it's also sometimes referred to as Kite Hill.

Taking the waters The type of water springing out of Hampstead Heath varies depending upon the local geology. Where Bagshot sands are present, the water is iron-rich and is known as chalybeate. In other places west of the Heath, the water is softer and lime-free. Both have therapeutic values and became much prized during the 18th century. Those Londoners who could afford it would flock to Hampstead to 'take the waters', thought its quality as drinking water left much to be desired. However, establishments were created to supply the efficacious liquid and offer entertainment such as dancing and firework displays.

The wealthy would also send their dirty linen up to Hampstead to be washed in the waters and, if weather conditions allowed, it would be tried on the Heath gorse bushes, giving off the fragrance of honey and coconut. As such, several Hampstead streets were appropriately named, including Well Road, Flask Walk and Well Walk.

5 Ruth Ellis The pavement outside the Magdala pub was where Ruth Ellis shot her lover dead in April 1955. In the subsequent trial she was found guilty and sentenced to death. She was hanged at HMP Holloway and became the last female in the UK to die in such a manner.

6 Royal Free Hospital As you walk further south over the Heath the looming presence of the Royal Free Hospital becomes more apparent. This infirmary was founded in Holborn in 1828 by the surgeon William Marsden as a free hospital for those who could not afford to pay for health care. It gained its 'royal' status nine years later. Despite the hospital expanding several times throughout the 19th century, by the 1960s the building was too small and inefficient to provide good care. A new hospital was built on Pond Street, Hampstead, opening in 1974.

Left: a view from Parliament Hill of the City of London, St Paul's Cathedral and the Shard. Top right: a diver takes the plunge at the Kenwood Ladies' Bathing Pond.

PRIMROSE HILL – REGENT'S PARK

Total walking distance 7.6km

The Royal Parks Primrose Hill and Regent's Park are separated by the Regent's Canal. Both were once part of the huge forest that covered a swathe of north London. Then teeming with boar, wild bulls and deer, this area was one of Henry VIII's favourite hunting grounds. Today, both parks are hugely popular open green spaces for walking, picnics and sporting activities.

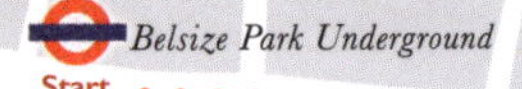

The neighbourhood The surrounding areas of St John's Wood, Swiss Cottage and Chalk Farm began to develop as affluent residential districts from the 1820s onwards. Many of the original stucco and brick terraced houses still stand and the areas are renowned for chic shops, upmarket restaurants and gastro pubs.

1 The murder of Edmund Godfrey The body of Edmund Godfrey JP was found in a ditch at the base of Primrose Hill in October 1678. But he was dead long before his body was dumped here.

Godfrey had been commissioned to investigate a Catholic plot to overthrow Charles II. Following the publication of his report he began to fear for his life. An investigation into his murder led to the arrest of Miles Prance, a Catholic, who under interrogation offered up the names of Green, Berry and Hill; three Catholics he maintained were the murderers. During the trial Prance's evidence was shown to be dubious and he withdrew it. Regardless, the three accused were sentenced to death and hung at Tyburn. The real perpetrators were never found.

2 Primrose Hill The view from the top of Primrose Hill is quite exceptional. Although only 63m above sea level it is central London's natural viewing point.

Immediately to the south is London Zoo and Regent's Park and farther beyond is Canary Wharf, the City and the Shard. Nestling between the latter two is St Paul's Cathedral. Seventy years ago, this structure dominated the London skyline but is now overwhelmed by office tower blocks. However, the view of St Paul's is protected from here, and many other viewpoints around London.

Prior to mid-16th century the hill was tree-covered. During the reign of Elizabeth I, this area, including what is now Regent's Park, was cleared of trees to make way for smallholdings (agriculture would provide

the royal treasury with a much better income).

The poet, painter and printmaker William Blake (1757–1827) would often walk up to the top of Primrose Hill and was no doubt inspired by the view he saw. Around the time Blake was frequenting the hill, Welsh Druids would assemble here to celebrate the solstice and equinox periods. Stirred by these events, Blake wrote 'I have conversed with the spiritual sun. I saw him on Primrose Hill'. The quote has now been inscribed on York stone edging placed at the highest point of the hill.

During the Second World War, given the uninterrupted views from the top of the hill, anti-aircraft guns were installed here to protect London. In the fictional *The War of the Worlds* by HG Wells, the author planned that the Martians would use the hill as their headquarters.

3 Friedrich Engels

The German political philosopher, industrialist and political theorist Friedrich Engels (1820–1895) lived for almost the last third of his life at 122 Regent's Park Road, until 1894. Engels worked closely with fellow German philosopher, Karl Marx and together they published several influential works, most famous of which was *The Communist Manifesto* (1848). Engels also provided financial assistance to Marx, which enabled the research, writing and publication of *Das Kapital* (1867).

A bloody prediction In the mid-16th century a Yorkshire-born soothsayer, Ursula Sontheil, better known as Mother Shipton (1488–1561), predicted that if Primrose Hill, then enclosed by farms and woods, became surrounded by London, the streets of the capital would run with blood. The hill is now very much bounded by London but fortunately the prediction has yet to occur.

Right: Friedrich Engels. Below left: the panoramic view of Regent's Park and London beyond from Primrose Hill.

***1* Regent's Park** The Manor of Tyburn (part of which is now Regent's Park) was owned by the Abbess of Barking, but in 1549 these and many other ecclesiastical estates were seized by Henry VIII during the Reformation. A hundred years later during the Civil War, over 16,000 trees were recorded in this location prior to many being felled for ship-building and the land cleared to create smallholdings. Most of those trees were never replaced.

In the mid-18th century a new toll road was created between Paddington and the City of London (it would later be known as Marylebone Road). It ran along the southern end of what would become Regent's Park.

London was expanding and more green space was needed to build new homes. The Crown Estates knew that more money could be made from the development of property rather than farming. A competition was held to not only remodel the park but to create a new boulevard (Regent Street) to connect St James's Park to Regent's Park. The architect and planner John Nash had been appointed 'Surveyor General of Woods Forests Parks and Chases' or manager of the Crown Estates in 1806. And it was his proposal that won the competition, plans for 56 stuccoed villas dotted around the new park, two circular roads, a lake and a canal passing through the estate. Nash had the ear of the Prince Regent (later George IV) and repaid him with the suggestion of naming the park, boulevard and canal after his title.

However, all did not progress as Nash would have liked. Only eight villas were built within the park, and the canal, of which Nash was a director, was forced to loop around the northern edge of the park, hidden within an embankment. However, a number of fine Regency terraced houses were constructed around the perimeter of the park, many of which are still standing today.

Nash went on to design many of London's best-known architectural features including Buckingham Palace and Marble Arch. Today, Regent's Park is 160ha in size and, unlike Hampstead Heath to the north, it is a well-manicured piece of green open space.

2 ZSL London Zoo The Zoological Society of London (ZSL) was established in 1826. One of the leading proponents of a zoo within the park was the botanist and zoologist Sir Thomas Stamford Raffles (Raffles had helped establish the Singapore colony). Plans for a zoo and research facilities were then drawn up by Decimus Burton and it opened in 1830, although was only accessible to ZSL members, while fee-paying visitors were finally admitted from 1847. The zoo quickly became a huge success with the public. The world's first Reptile House opened here in 1849 and over the years more exotic animals and reptiles have been displayed. A new Modernist penguin pool was designed in 1936 by the architects Lubetkin and Tecton. At the outbreak of the Second World War many animals had to be evacuated to the sister zoo, Whipsnade in Bedfordshire, for their safety. The Snowdon Aviary, visible from the canal towpath, was designed by Anthony Armstrong Jones (Lord Snowdon) with Cedric Price and Frank Newby, and was opened in 1965. The ZSL plays a large part in the preservation and protection of endangered animals around the world, and income from admission fees and sponsorship still pays for the research today.

3 The Readymoney Drinking Fountain This ornate Neo-Gothic water fountain was donated in 1869 by the Parsi philanthropist and businessman Sir Cowasjee Jehangir Readymoney. The fountain, constructed of Aberdeen granite and marble, stands in the centre of the Broad Walk. 'Readymoney' was a nickname given to Jehangir, which he later implemented as a surname. Sadly, it is no longer a working drinking fountain.

4 Queen Mary's Rose Garden This outstanding landscaped rose garden was named after the wife of George V and opened in 1934. With over 12,000 rose bushes (85 single species), 9,000 begonias, a fountain and an exquisite Mediterranean garden. It is the largest formal rose garden in London.

5 Regent's Park Open Air Theatre This outdoor theatre was established in 1932 with a capacity of 1,256 seats, making it one of London's largest theatrical venues.

6 The Bandstand Bombing On 20 July 1982, seven military bandsmen were killed (one later succumbing to his injuries) when a bomb planted beneath the bandstand exploded. The performance had gone ahead despite a similar attack that morning in Hyde Park. While the Provisional IRA claimed responsibility for both attacks, no one has ever been charged with the Regent's Park killings.

Clockwise from left: a giraffe outside its enclosure; The Readymoney Drinking Fountain; Queen Mary's Rose Garden.

1 The Holme This Regency house overlooking the boating lake was designed by the young Decimus Burton (aged 18) for his father James, in 1818. James Burton was responsible for the design of many houses in Bloomsbury and St Johns Wood. D Burton went on to design many of the buildings within Regent's Park including Hanover Lodge, Grove House and the zoo's Giraffe House. He would become best known for the layout of the Royal Botanic Gardens in Kew along with the design of the Palm and Temperate houses within.

2 The Boating Lake This human-made lake, once filled with water from the subterranean River Tyburn, is a very popular boating lake in the summer. However, it was once the scene of a major disaster. During the winter of 1867, the lake froze over and it became a popular destination for ice skaters. On 15 January, following a brief thaw in the temperature, the ice cracked and around 200 people fell in to the freezing water. Attempts to remain buoyant while wearing heavy skates proved difficult for many and 40 people drowned that day.

3 Winfield House The first house to occupy this location was Hertford Villa, designed by Decimus Burton in 1825. It was part of the master plan for the newly laid out Regent's Park. In 1936, Barbara Hutton, granddaughter of Frank Winfield Woolworth and heiress of the Woolworth store empire, acquired the decaying villa and had it entirely rebuilt in a red brick Georgian style and renamed it Winfield House. During the Second World War, the house was requisitioned by the RAF as a barrage balloon storage facility and it was damaged by nearby bombing activity. After the war, Hutton sold the building to the US government for a dollar. It was again restored, and from 1955, it became home to US ambassadors.

4 The Hub This circular structure is the centre of the largest sports facility in London and provides underground changing rooms. Regent's Park plays host to many sporting activities including football, cricket, rugby, lacrosse and softball.

5 Macclesfield Bridge This bridge over the Regent's Canal (page 80) was accidentally destroyed in October 1874. A barge by the name of *Tilbury*, containing 5 tons of gunpowder, was being towed along the canal, with another four barges, one of which contained barrels of petroleum. A spark from the engine's fire of the *Ready*, a steam-powered tugboat heading the procession, may have ignited the petroleum and gunpowder, causing a massive explosion that killed the three crew and destroyed Macclesfield Bridge. Windows up to 1.5km away were smashed and *Tilbury's* keel was later located in a basement 300m away. Such was the commercial value of the canal that it was repaired and back in operation within five days. The bridge is sometimes referred to as Blow Up Bridge.

6 Chalbert Footbridge This footbridge conceals a conduit that carries the subterranean River Tyburn over the Regent's Canal.

7 The Terry Mansions At first glance these six detached mansions appear to have been constructed during the 17th and 18th centuries. However, construction of the villas, designed by classical architects

Quinlan and Francis Terry, commenced in 1988, with each villa being a pastiche of a particular European architectural styling.

8 Central London Mosque In 1940, King George VI donated an acre of Crown Estate in Regent's Park, in exchange for land in Egypt (to build an Anglican church) for the specific use of creating a new London mosque. Prior to this time no such place of Muslim worship existed in central London. The British government contributed £100,000 to the cost of building. However, it took another 37 years to finish the project. The finished mosque, which opened in 1977, can accommodate 5,000 worshippers. The golden dome and minaret are now an integral part of the Regent's Park skyline.

Clockwise from far left: the Regent's Park boating lake with the Regency residence The Holme; Macclesfield Bridge, rebuilt following an accidental explosion in 1874; the Central London Mosque; a Canadian goose, a common sight in the park.

Page opposite: a view from Alexandra Palace over north London and the City.

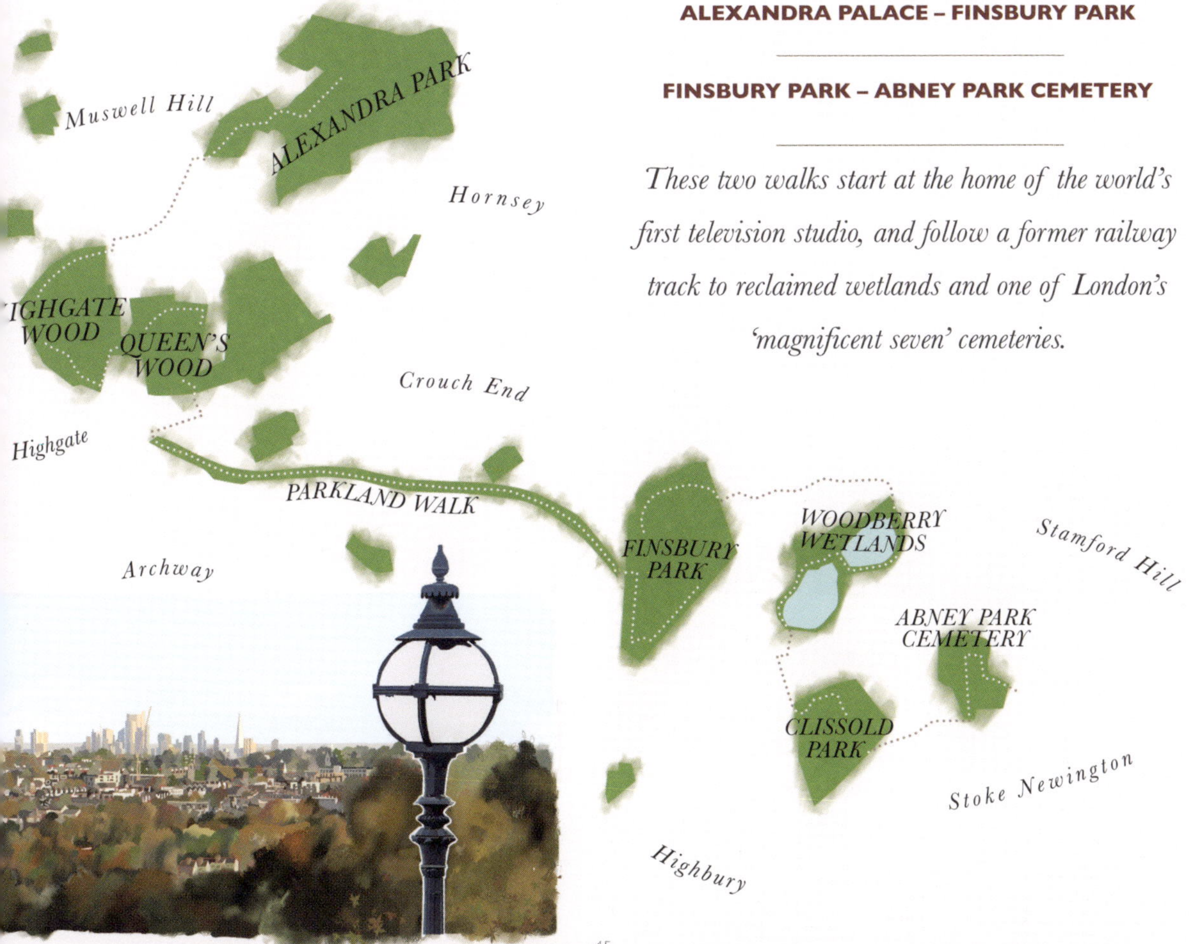

ALEXANDRA PALACE – FINSBURY PARK

FINSBURY PARK – ABNEY PARK CEMETERY

These two walks start at the home of the world's first television studio, and follow a former railway track to reclaimed wetlands and one of London's 'magnificent seven' cemeteries.

ALEXANDRA PALACE – FINSBURY PARK

Total walking distance 9.6km

This walk, mainly along an old railway line, is almost entirely traffic-free. The route, which in places follows the Capital Ring, encompasses an ancient wood, a popular leisure venue, the site of the world's first television broadcast and the final residence of a 20th-century mass murderer.

1 Alexandra Palace The Great Exhibition of 1851 in Hyde Park (page 18) ushered in a trend for industrialised nations to showcase to the world the advances they were making in industry, science and the arts. In 1860, a plan was put in place by the architect Owen Jones, who had worked on the Great Exhibition project to create a large exhibition centre and a leisure park on the Northern Heights, above Hornsey. Alexandra Palace was an Italianate structure, partially created from building materials salvaged from the 1862 International Exhibition in South Kensington.

A railway track from Finsbury Park was installed in time for the opening of Alexandra Palace on 24 May 1873, by Princess Alexandra, the Princess of Wales. The Palace attracted over 100,000 visitors before it was badly damaged by fire only 16 days after its opening. But such was the enthusiasm for the complex that it was repaired and reopened two years later.

The Palace, now often referred to as 'Ally Pally' or the People's Palace, stands on a 3ha site and included at its inception a large hall, a concert room, a restaurant and a theatre. Amenities within the 90ha Alexandra Park included a horse racing track (which remained operational until 1970), a cricket field and a boating pond. The park also became famous for its firework and hot-air balloon displays. Regardless of these attractions, the palace and park were not a financial success and by 1901 it was placed under the control of the local council. Since 1980, it has been managed by Alexandra Park and Palace Charitable Trust, with Haringey Council being the sole trustee.

During the First World War, the Palace accommodated Belgian refugees (1,000 beds were packed into the Great Hall) and from 1915 it became an internment camp for German prisoners of war plus 17,000 Germans and Austrians living in Britain who were seen as a threat to security.

In 1980, the Palace burned down for a second time after a fire started beneath the organ. Again, the building was repaired, and it reopened eight years later. The redesigned structure included an ice rink that added to its list of attractions. The Great Hall still features popular events such as music concerts, international darts tournaments, beer festivals and exhibitions. Today, the park, with over 7,000 trees, features a children's zip-wire playground, a boating pond with giant swan pedalos, a pitch-and-putt golf course and a farmer's market. Fantastic views of London can be seen from the South Terrace walkway.

Left: the south elevation of Alexandra Palace. Above right: Muffin the Mule, a children's programme, first broadcast from the BBC Studios at Alexandra Palace.

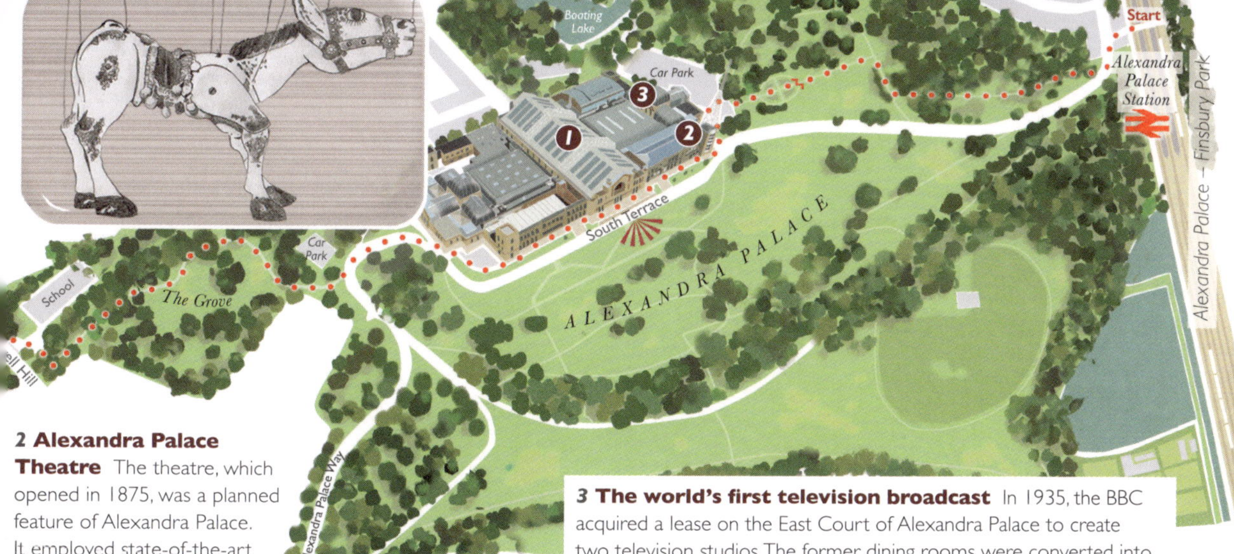

2 Alexandra Palace Theatre

The theatre, which opened in 1875, was a planned feature of Alexandra Palace. It employed state-of-the-art Victorian technology to present plays and musical entertainment to audiences of up to 3,000. The theatre closed during the First World War and didn't reopen until 1922. One of its post-war impresarios was Archie Pitt, the first husband of Gracie Fields. Fields was to become a very popular British actress of stage and film. One of her most famous theatre productions *The Show's The Thing* debuted at Alexandra Palace Theatre before heading to the West End. Despite this and other productions, the theatre struggled to attract large audiences and it closed in 1935. Soon after, it was acquired by the BBC and became a storeroom.

The theatre suffered much damage and decay over eight decades and an extensive restoration programme was needed to bring it back to life. In 2018, with financial support from the Heritage Lottery Fund and Haringey Council, the theatre was finally reopened.

3 The world's first television broadcast

In 1935, the BBC acquired a lease on the East Court of Alexandra Palace to create two television studios. The former dining rooms were converted into experimental TV studios. The BBC began trialling two rival systems at Alexandra Palace to decide which option would be chosen to transmit the world's first regular 'high definition' television broadcast. The team, headed by Sir Isaac Shoenberg of Marconi-EMI, beat the (John Logie) Baird Company and the first broadcast was transmitted from Alexandra Palace on 2 November 1936, with a variety show entitled *Here's Looking at You*. The transmitter was located on the roof of the building. All the initial broadcasts went out live. A live transmission of the coronation of King George VI, in December 1936, was only made possible by a cable that ran from Hyde Park to the studios at Alexandra Palace.

The BBC also transmitted the first children's television programme *For the Children* from the Alexandra Palace studios in 1946. It featured a wooden puppet, Muffin the Mule, who went on to be very popular with children and their parents. The BBC television news continued to be broadcast from here until 1969.

Walking these pages 2.1km

1 Parkland Walk North Once out of The Grove, the footpath passes Muswell Hill Primary School and heads, via a pedestrian tunnel, under the carriageway (Muswell Hill) to the beginning of the northern section of the Parkland Walk. It is a short (700m) prelude to the Parkland Walk beyond Highgate Underground Station. The walk offers more stunning views over sections of London and beyond. In the time since the railway track was closed in the 1950s and the track removed, the trees have grown to form a natural tunnel over the pathway. This section of the Parkland Walk doesn't connect directly to the southern leg of the route but it can be accessed through Highgate and Queen's Wood.

2 The Muswell Hill serial killer In early 1983, after several occupants at 23 Cranley Gardens complained of a blocked drain, a plumber was called to fix the problem. What he found obstructing the pipe were possible human remains, and the police were called. A forensic examination revealed that these were the body parts of a young male. The top-floor tenant, Dennis Nilsen, a civil servant, was questioned by the police and he immediately confessed to killing the man. He also admitted to murdering at least two other men at this address and nine at his previous address in Cricklewood, north-west London. Nilsen picked up young, often homeless, homosexual men and invited them back to his flat for food and alcohol. Having intoxicated his victim, he would usually strangle and then drown them in the bath. In Cricklewood, he buried the bodies under the floorboards of his ground-floor flat before cremating the remains in the garden. This wasn't possible in the top-floor flat at Cranley Gardens without access to a garden. Instead he dismembered the bodies, boiled up the fragments and flushed the smaller bones down the toilet. Nilsen was tried at the Old Bailey, found guilty and was sentenced to life imprisonment, although this was later changed to a whole-life tariff. He died in prison in 2018.

3 Highgate Wood
This richly wooded area, once known as Gravelpit Wood, is a small section (28ha) of the former ancient Forest of Middlesex. Today, the wood, despite being enclosed by Muswell Hill Road and the A1, is a quiet haven for walkers. The forest was once used by the Bishops of London to hunt deer. From the 16th to the 18th century the wood was leased out to tenants who coppiced the trees to supply wood for fuel, fencing and building. Coppicing involved cutting the tree back to encourage new growth for later harvesting. Trees such as oak and hornbeam are still plentiful in Highgate Wood, and were a good source of such material.

Pottery and kiln remains from the Romano-Briton era have been unearthed and dated at between AD 50 and AD 100. There is still evidence of a woodbank (or earthwork) cutting across the woods. This was a small wall of earth with bushes planted along the top and a ditch on one side (*marked with a white broken line on the map*). It may have been created to protect the wooded areas being eaten by deer in search of low-hanging leaves.

When the railway line was constructed around the wood in 1873, locals were concerned that it might be built over with houses. Following a campaign to prevent this, Ecclesiastical Commissioners handed the wood over to the City of London Corporation in 1886 for use by the public in perpetuity. It has since been designated a Site of Metropolitan Importance for Nature Conservation. During the Second World War barrage balloons were stationed on the cricket pitch.

4 Peter Sellers The comic actor and Goon Peter Sellers (1925–1980) lived here from 1936 for four years. A plaque marks the house.

5 Queen's Wood Unlike the flat terrain of Highgate Wood, Queen's Wood is situated on sloping terrain. This wood, too, was once part of the ancient Forest of Middlesex and used as a hunting ground. Oaks were plentiful here and farmers paid the Bishop of London a fee to graze their pigs upon the acorns. This woodland was formerly known as Churchyard Bottom Wood.

As London continued to expand through the 19th century, the Ecclesiastical Commissioners did consider selling off the wood for housing development. Local residents resisted, and succeeded in getting the local council to acquire the wood and make it accessible to all. The wood was opened to the public in 1898 and was renamed Queen's Wood in honour of Queen Victoria's Golden Jubilee of that year. A small stream rises in the wood and during wet periods can be seen flowing eastward. This stream merges with several other tributaries to form the River Moselle. The name Moselle is probably a corruption of Muswell (Hill) or Mossy Well.

Clockwise from far left: the serial killer Dennis Nilsen; the ornate metal entrance at Cranley Gate; a hornbeam tree with a leaf detail.

1 Uncle Adolf In 1930, a mother and her son moved into 26 Priory Gardens. She had been abandoned by her husband some sixteen years earlier. While this may have created some local gossip, it was nothing compared to discovering the family surname was Hitler. Bridget Dowling had married Adolf Hitler's half-brother, Alois, in London in 1910 and their son, William was born a year later. As Adolf Hitler rose to power during the 1930s, Alois renewed contact with his half-brother. Meanwhile, Willy, wanting to reunite with his father in Germany, joined him in 1933, and thanks to the family surname and connections was soon able to find work. But as the rush towards war gathered pace, Willy returned to Priory Gardens in 1939. The same year, he and his mother were invited to America to give a lecture tour on life with the Hitler family. Trapped there by the outbreak of the Second World War, Willy was awarded American citizenship. He ended up joining the US Navy and fought against the Nazis.

2 Bat caves After descending down the slope from Holmesdale Road into Parkland Walk, turn immediately left and head towards the former railway tunnels. The tunnels, now sealed off with railings, provide a safe sanctuary for seven breeds of bats, including the common pipistrelle, the Daubenton and the Natterer. The Parkland Walk is also a natural feeding and roosting strip for the bats. The adjacent wooded areas, such as Finsbury Park, Highgate and Queen's Wood, also have bat populations that are linked by the Parkland Walk. Many bats roost in the trees, under the bridges and in human-made bat boxes.

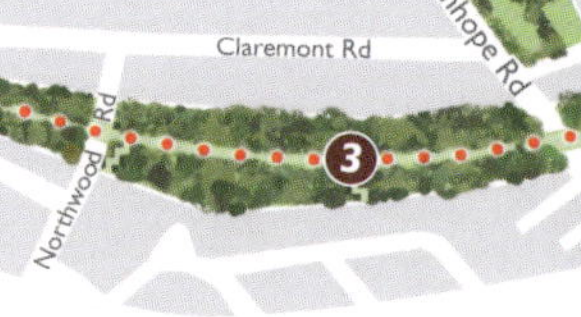

Clockwise from lower left: a redundant railway tunnel, now home to several species of bats; a Spriggan sculpture within the railway arches; a section of the Parkland Walk close to The Spriggan.

3 Parkland Walk The Parkland Walk was opened to the public in 1984 after much campaigning and discussion about what to do with the former railway track. The Edgware, Highgate and London Railway opened in 1867 with a branch to Alexandra Palace opening five years later.

In the 1930s, a plan was proposed to electrify the line and to integrate it with the Underground network. The scheme was partially completed, with the track from Highgate to Barnet being electrified. The outbreak of war in 1939 ceased all further development. The track to Edgware was only updated as far as Mill Hill East and it remains a spur on the Northern line. The train service to Alexandra Palace was discontinued after 1954, though the track continued to be

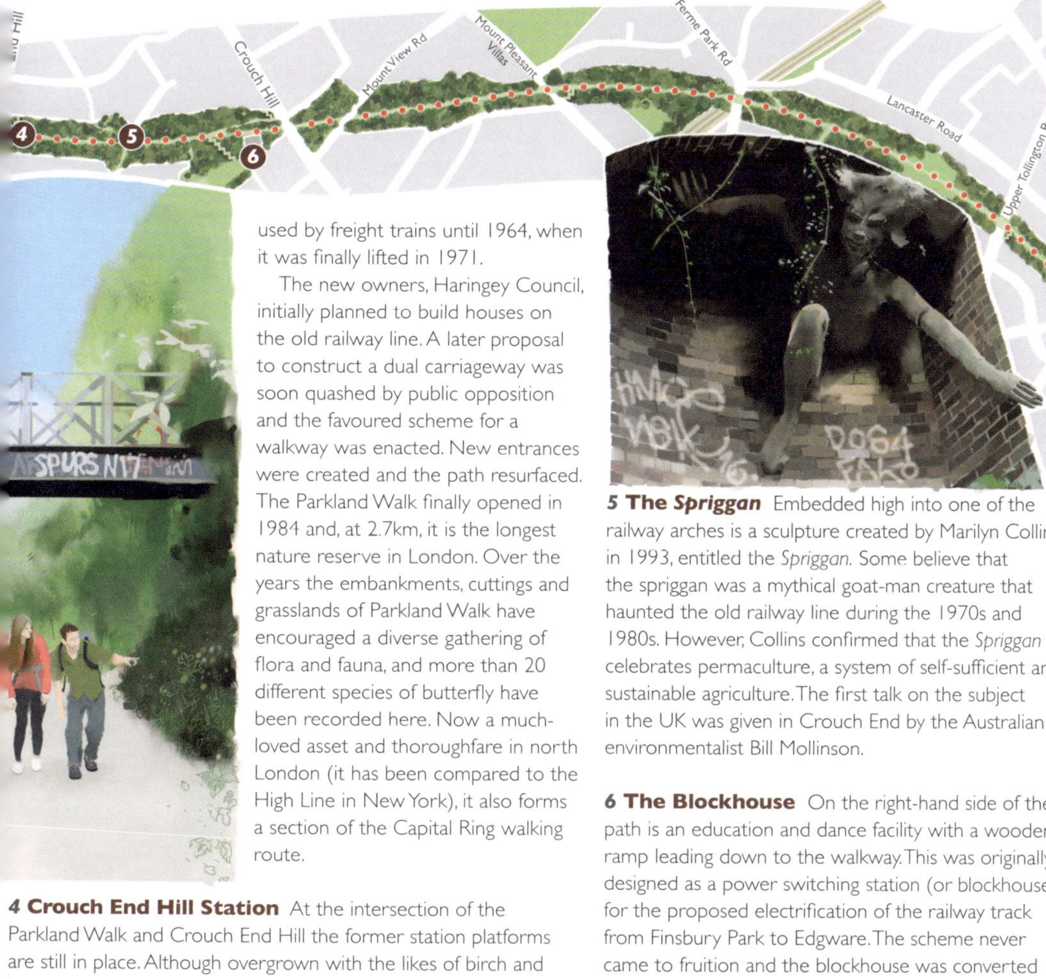

used by freight trains until 1964, when it was finally lifted in 1971.

The new owners, Haringey Council, initially planned to build houses on the old railway line. A later proposal to construct a dual carriageway was soon quashed by public opposition and the favoured scheme for a walkway was enacted. New entrances were created and the path resurfaced. The Parkland Walk finally opened in 1984 and, at 2.7km, it is the longest nature reserve in London. Over the years the embankments, cuttings and grasslands of Parkland Walk have encouraged a diverse gathering of flora and fauna, and more than 20 different species of butterfly have been recorded here. Now a much-loved asset and thoroughfare in north London (it has been compared to the High Line in New York), it also forms a section of the Capital Ring walking route.

4 Crouch End Hill Station At the intersection of the Parkland Walk and Crouch End Hill the former station platforms are still in place. Although overgrown with the likes of birch and buddleia, the platforms remain apparent.

5 The *Spriggan* Embedded high into one of the railway arches is a sculpture created by Marilyn Collins in 1993, entitled the *Spriggan*. Some believe that the spriggan was a mythical goat-man creature that haunted the old railway line during the 1970s and 1980s. However, Collins confirmed that the *Spriggan* celebrates permaculture, a system of self-sufficient and sustainable agriculture. The first talk on the subject in the UK was given in Crouch End by the Australian environmentalist Bill Mollinson.

6 The Blockhouse On the right-hand side of the path is an education and dance facility with a wooden ramp leading down to the walkway. This was originally designed as a power switching station (or blockhouse) for the proposed electrification of the railway track from Finsbury Park to Edgware. The scheme never came to fruition and the blockhouse was converted into a community centre.

FINSBURY PARK – ABNEY PARK CEMETERY

Total walking distance 7.4km

This walk through two Victorian parks follows, in part, the route of a 400-year-old human-made water channel, reservoirs and the Capital Ring. It passes the location where the novel *Robinson Crusoe* was written and ends in the magnificent decaying splendour of Abney Park Cemetery.

1 Edward V Following the death of Edward IV in April 1483, his 12-year-old son, also called Edward, was escorted back to London for the funeral. The City of London authorities, keen to show loyalty to the new king, headed north to greet him. They met in Hornsey Wood, part of which would later become Finsbury Park. Edward V, under the supervision of his uncle Richard, was then housed in the Tower of London, along with his brother. Richard declared that the two brothers were illegitimate and that he was the rightful heir to the throne of England. He was crowned Richard III in June 1483 and the two brothers soon disappeared from public view. It is believed that their uncle had them murdered and the bodies disposed of.

2 Finsbury Park As the 19th century progressed and the population of London continued to expand, the demand for green open spaces, away from the smoke and grime, gathered pace. In 1845, Victoria Park had opened for those living in the East End. North of the City of London, the people of Finsbury were feeling increasingly overwhelmed by the lack of open spaces available for walking and exercing on their days off. A plan was proposed in 1851 to create another large park from Highbury Corner to what is now Finsbury Park, which would include Clissold Park. James Pennethorne, the designer of Victoria and Battersea Parks, was put in charge. The area was going to be called Albert Park in memory of Queen Victoria's late husband.

However, property developers had acquired much of the land to the south of Finsbury Park and the scheme was reduced in scale. Finsbury Park, formerly part of Hornsey Wood, was the southernmost section of the ancient Forest of Middlesex. Just south of the present lake in Finsbury Park stood a tearoom, named Hornsey Wood House (**2a**). The house became popular not only for its beverages but also for the provision

Right: the New River as it flows through Finsbury Park.
Below: a baseball match in Finsbury Park.

"

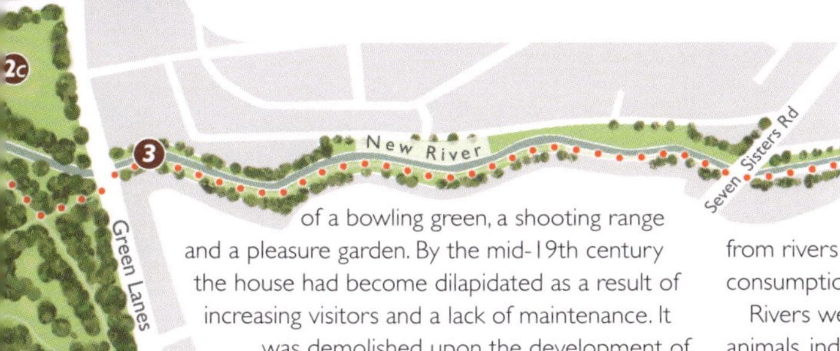

of a bowling green, a shooting range and a pleasure garden. By the mid-19th century the house had become dilapidated as a result of increasing visitors and a lack of maintenance. It was demolished upon the development of the new park.

In 1857, the Finsbury Park Act was passed to construct a new 46ha area of open parkland to the south of Hornsey. Finsbury Park was finally opened to the public 12 years later. The original lake was enlarged and water was supplied from the nearby New River. Several ornamental zones were created including the American Gardens. In the 20th century numerous features were added, including a children's play area, a café, a bowling green, an athletics track (**2b**) and a baseball diamond (home of the London Mets – **2c**).

The municipal park has changed hands several time and is now managed by the London Borough of Haringey. In 2003, a £5 million Heritage Lottery Fund donation helped to restore some of the park's run-down gardens and an outdoor gym was created. Several music events are held in the park, including the Wireless Festival. While such events are not always popular with the locals, as they close the park and destroy the grass in areas, the money raised is reinvested into the park's maintenance and infrastructure.

3 New River The title of this narrow waterway is misleading as it is no longer new nor a river. Rather, it is a 400-year-old human-made waterway for the supply of water into London. In 1600, the population of the capital was about 300,000 and growing. The supply of drinking water was haphazard; it usually came from rivers and wells, and it was rarely filtered or treated before consumption.

Rivers were also in demand as a waste disposal facility; dead animals, industrial waste and even human remains could end up in the streams. The rivers Fleet, Walbrook, Tyburn and Thames were increasingly becoming more polluted and potentially hazardous to drink from, although the connection between cholera and poor water supply had yet to be made.

In 1607, a plan was devised to carry water from two springs at Chadwell and Amwell in Hertfordshire into reservoirs at New River Head in Clerkenwell. This location was around 25m above the City, so water would then be gravity-fed, via wooden pipes, into City houses and public conduits. Two parliamentary acts were passed for this large, privately funded engineering plan to occur. Water would only be supplied to those who could afford the subscription.

The initial project collapsed financially after only a few miles of the New River had been dug. The project was then taken over by Sir Hugh Myddleton, MP and goldsmith. But Myddleton's New River Company was not immune to financial problems either. He appealed to James I, who owned a property on the proposed river route, and in return for half the profits, the monarch supplied 50 per cent of the capital. Having the King's backing for the project enabled the developers to overcome resistance by many landowners whose property would be carved up by the waterway. The 63km-long channel only dropped 6m on its journey to the Clerkenwell reservoirs. Although the waterway no longer reaches here, the New River still supplies London with 8 per cent of its daily water requirements (210 million litres).

I Stoke Newington Reservoirs In the 1820s, London continued expanding but was still getting much of its drinking water from unsafe sources. Two new reservoirs, totalling 21ha, were constructed in Stoke Newington and were fed directly by the New River. They were planned and designed by William Chadwell Mylne, the New River Company's chief civil engineer and architect. The water from these reservoirs was passed through filter beds in an attempt to purify it before consumption, and then they began to supply water to north London in 1833. The banks of the reservoirs were lined with stone from the recently demolished old London Bridge. Water continued to flow along the New River to the reservoirs in Clerkenwell until 1946. After this time, the New River, south of the Stoke Newington Reservoirs, was reduced in places to an ornamental water feature and in many areas was simply covered over.

2 Woodberry Wetlands In the early part of this century property developers had hoped to buy the East Reservoir, drain it and build upon the 12ha of land. However, local residents fiercely resisted the proposal and the plans were withdrawn. Instead, a wetland reserve was created by the London Wildlife Trust, on behalf of Thames Water. In 2016, the Woodberry Wetlands were opened to the public. The planting of reed beds has encouraged waterfowl such as bunting and reed warblers to nest and breed here. It has also become a resting space for migratory birds and is home to numerous other birds and wildlife, including kestrels, kingfishers and sparrow hawks. The Woodberry Wetlands includes a visitor centre and the Coal House Café (**2a**).

Clockwise from left: the gated entrance to Woodberry Wetlands at Newnton Close; an inscription on the northern side of the Coal House Café; a view across the Wetlands reed beds (featuring a reed warbler), looking towards St Mary's Church, Stoke Newington (page 57), the City of London and the Shard.

N
Walking these
pages 1.0km

_1_ The West Reservoir Centre

The West Reservoir is now used for various supervised water sports, including kayaking, sailing and swimming. The former filter beds and station now form the sailing club house and café.

2 The Castle Climbing Centre

Standing at the southern end of the reservoirs and by Green Lanes is an oddly located castle. This structure once contained the steam-powered pumps to raise water up into the water tower. Following the 1852 Metropolis Water Act, water could no longer be extracted from the Thames as it had become too polluted. Dr John Snow had made a break-through discovery in 1849, that tainted water supplies could be the carrier of cholera. Water now had to be extracted from healthy sources, such as the wells of Hertfordshire. The New River Company and William Chadwell Mylne commissioned Robert Billings to design this Scottish baronial castle to house the pumping engines. In 1946, diesel pumps replaced the steam engines and later the building became surplus to requirements. In 1995, it reopened as The Castle Climbing Centre.

3 Green Lanes This lane was once an ancient cattle droving route. Animals were herded over many miles towards Smithfield Market to be sold and slaughtered for their meat. In places there were multiple tracks so that the different herds couldn't mix; hence the plural name 'Lanes'.

4 Clissold Park Within the grounds of Clissold Park is a building once named Paradise House. The house, with its six Doric-columned portico, was created in the late 18th century for Jonathan Hoare, a Quaker and brother of the anti-enslavement campaigner Samuel Hoare. Stoke Newington had, by the mid-19th century, the largest Quaker community in London. So, it was hardly surprising that the non-conformist cemetery, Abney Park, would be created here.

In 1811, the house was leased to William Crawshay. Crawshay's daughter Elizabeth, despite her father's objections, began secretly dating the local vicar, the Reverend Augustus Clissold. They were only able to marry following the death of her father, at which point Clissold moved into Paradise House and modestly renamed it after himself. By 1886, the house and the estate were put up for sale and plans made to build new private residences upon it. Local public resistance was roused, and a campaign ensued to save the estate for public use. Earlier plans had been considered to include the grounds within a larger Albert Park (page 52).

The estate and its house were saved and eventually opened to the public in 1889. The two ponds that had been created when clay was dug to make bricks for the house, were filled with water from the New River. They are named Beck and Runtz after two of the leading campaigners who saved the estate for the public. The were once filled with water from the Hackney Brook, a stream that once flowed around the northern perimeter of the park, though it is now a subterranean waterway. The long, curving lake within the park was also was once a section of the New River before it was terminated at the reservoirs in 1946.

Today, Clissold House (**4a**) is a fine café and the 23ha ground contains a deer park (**4b**), a butterfly dome, several football pitches, tennis courts and a cricket

Clockwise from right: Clissold House, a former residential house, now a cafe; St Mary's Church; the former pumping station, now The Castle Climbing Centre on Green Lanes.

pitch. The park features several exotic trees including a dawn redwood, ginkgo, holm elm, Judas tree and black walnut, plus the more common ash, lime and oak trees.

5 St Mary's Old Church In the easternmost corner of Clissold Park sits the old St Mary's Church. There is a record of a church located here in 1314. It was rebuilt in 1563 and was at the time the village church, surrounded by countryside and a scattering of houses along Church Street. This Elizabethan church is the only one of its kind remaining in London. Augustus Clissold was a curate here. The ancient building is now an arts venue. Buried in the graveyard is James Stephen, a leading figure in the battle against enslavement and brother-in-law of William Wilberforce.

6 St Mary's Church In the 19th century, Stoke Newington lost its village status, as it was subsumed by the sprawling capital. The old church was no longer large enough to accommodate all the Sunday congregants, so a new church, St Mary's, was designed by Sir George Gilbert Scott in the Gothic Revival style and built upon the site of the old rectory, to the south of the old church. It was consecrated in 1858 with the large, 77m-tall spire being added in 1890.

1 **Stoke Newington Town Hall** Opened in 1937, this symmetrical, round-fronted civic building of Portland stone and brick was once home to Stoke Newington Metropolitan Borough Council. During the Second World War the building was used as a civic defence headquarters and was given a zebra stripe-style camouflage to help protect it from aerial attack. The faded paintwork is still just visible on the bricks today.

Following local government boundary changes in 1965, Stoke Newington became part of the London Borough of Hackney and the building, no longer required for council meetings, fell into disrepair. In 2010, the hall with its Art Deco details, was carefully restored and reopened as a community centre, with multifunctional facilities for such events as weddings, tea dances and theatre.

2 Robinson Crusoe In 1719, the author, journalist and non-conformist Daniel Defoe wrote the novel *Robinson Crusoe* in a house at this location, on the corner of Stoke Newington Church Street and Defoe Road. A plaque marks the spot. The novel was first published in 1719.

Notable Abney Park Cemetery graves

A **William Booth**, founder of the Salvation Army, and his wife **Catherine Booth**.

B London Fire Brigade Superintendent **James Braidwood**, who was killed in a huge London fire in 1861.

C **Joanna Vassa**, daughter of Olaudah Equiano, a former enslaved person and anti-enslavement campaigner.

D **Dr Isaac Watts**, a minister and hymn writer. He lived on this estate before it became a cemetery.

E **Commonwealth War Memorial**.

F **PC William Tyler**, a policeman killed while chasing armed robbers across north London in 1909. The incident became known as the 'Tottenham Outrage'.

G The sleeping lion, the grave and memorial of **Frank Bostock**, animal tamer and showman.

Stoke Newington Station 150m

Clockwise from bottom left: a plaque marking the site of Daniel Defoe's former house on Defoe Road; Stoke Newington Town Hall; Frank Bostock's grave in Abney Park Cemetery; the main cemetery gates on Stoke Newington High Street.

3 Abney Park Cemetery In 1832, Parliament passed a bill to encourage the creation of new private cemeteries beyond central London. The population of Greater London had increased by 70 per cent in 30 years and now stood at 1.7 million. The graveyards of the capital were full to bursting and more cemeteries were urgently needed.

The Abney Park Cemetery Company was founded by George Collison II with a plan to create the first non-denominational cemetery in Europe, and intended as a burial space for dissenters, or those practicing religion outside the established church.

The architect and planner William Hoskins was commissioned to convert the 12.5ha of land into a garden cemetery with a non-denominational Gothic chapel within the grounds. Hoskins also designed the grand Egyptian entrance gates on Stoke Newington High Street. The grounds of the cemetery had once been owned by Sir Thomas Abney, who in 1700 was the City of London mayor.

Trees were initially planted around the perimeter of the cemetery in (Latin) alphabetical order, from azer to zanthoxylum. The Hackney Brook formed the northern boundary of the park until it was culverted. The first burial occurred in 1840 and it was planned that around 120,000 bodies would be interred here. However, with a need to keep the cemetery financially viable, more bodies were squeezed in and the figure now stands at around 200,000. Eventually the Company declared bankruptcy and Abney Park was bought by the London Borough of Hackney in 1978, for £1. The cemetery is now run by the Abney Park Trust. Although managed and landscaped, the burial grounds, with some 2,500 trees, retain a wonderfully overgrown atmosphere.

Walking these pages 1.3km

Opposite: a view of London Stadium and Waterworks River from the Eastcross Bridge.

NORTH-EAST LONDON

THE LOWER LEE VALLEY

This is a walk along canals, rivers and reservoirs, over former marshlands that lead to the capital's newest green space: the Queen Elizabeth Olympic Park.

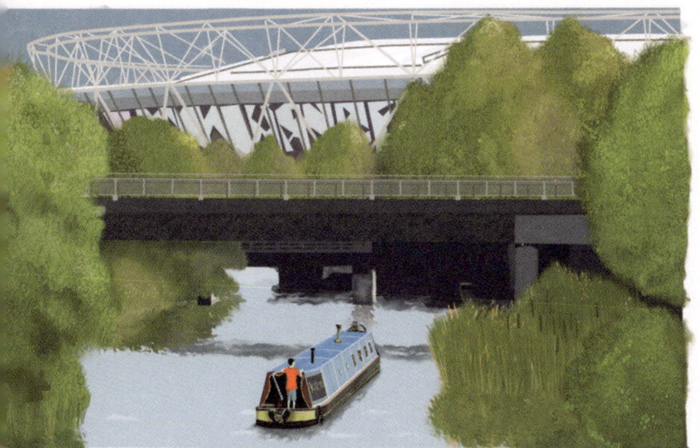

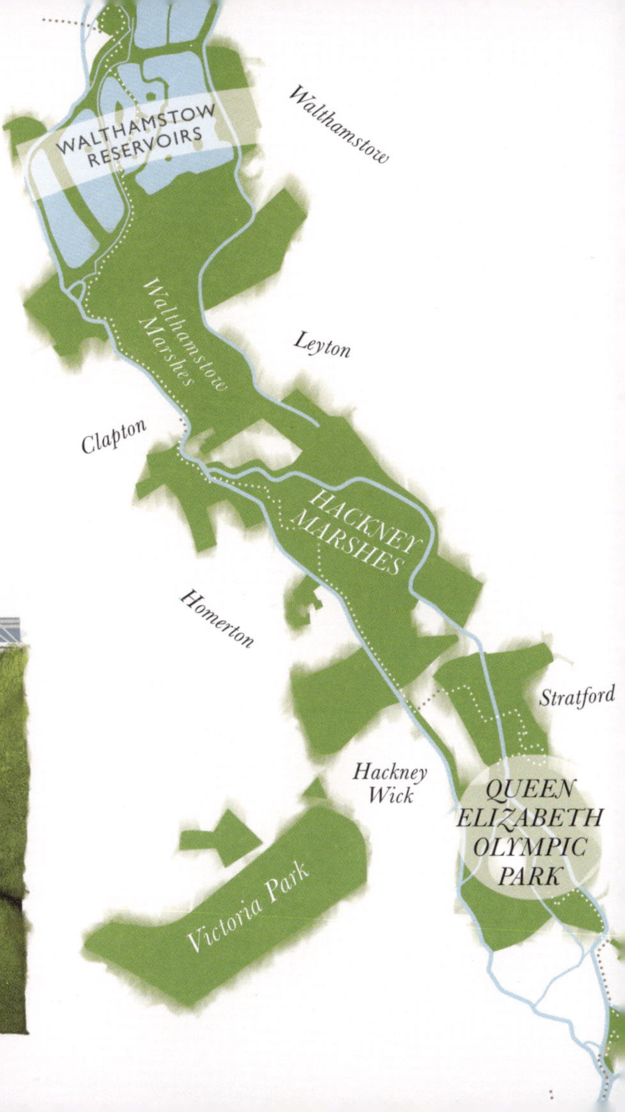

THE LOWER LEE VALLEY

Total walking distance 13.7km

This walk, along a former industrial water highway, has seen a great deal of restoration and transformation, much of it for the better.

After the River Thames, this waterway is historically, probably the most important stream in London. Not only was it a vital trade link, bringing foodstuffs and materials into the capital, but it also supplied drinking water to its inhabitants. The river was so important that during the 18th century a second channel had to be dug to allow increased transportation and support the growing number of watermills along its banks.

The awarding of the 2012 Olympic Games to London initiated a major clean-up. The 'stink-works' were moved out and the Lower Lea Valley was redeveloped to include new transport hubs, a shopping centre and sports arenas.

Below left: a fishing pier overlooking Reservoir No 1. Below right: the Engine House (a former pumping station), now the Walthamstow Wetlands visitor centre and café

***1* The River Lee Navigation** In 1761, the Bridgewater Canal opened in the north-west of England to make the transportation of coal more efficient, and thus began a mania for canal building. In 1776, an Act of Parliament was passed to improve the efficiency of the River Lea by canalising part of the stream and adding an additional, parallel waterway, known as the River Lee Navigation. Tottenham Lock was a part of this development.

The River Lea was for many hundreds of years a vital conduit for moving foodstuffs and raw material down from Hertfordshire and Essex into the capital. However, the lower section of the Lea was tidal and low rainfall could make the river less reliable at times. In the late 12th century, the Abbott of Waltham began making improvements to the Lea by adding a new channel. An Act of Parliament in 1424 added further channels, but it wasn't until the Act of 1766 that a master plan for the whole river was evident.

Flash locks were often installed along the Lea. These ancient, single-gate locks had to be opened to allow a boat through and then the gate quickly closed behind. Boats heading upstream had to be hauled through the lock as quickly as possible, to prevent heavy loss of water. These old locks were removed and replaced with double-gated locks such as the one at Tottenham. The entire River Lee Navigation is nearly 50km long.

2 Paddock Community Nature Park

These grounds were once part of Mill Mead water meadow. Following the First World War, the space was transformed into a sports field for the staff of the nearby Harris Lebus furniture factory. When the company was liquidated in 1969, the sports field fell into disrepair. In 2000, with the assistance of Haringey Council, the park opened to the public.

3 Ferry Boat Inn

Prior to 1760, the only way to cross the River Lea, at this point, was by ferry. That year, a bridge was built over this narrow section of the stream. Once the plan to create the River Lea Navigation was enacted, this bridge became vital for bringing in labour and materials. The 17th-century Grade-II listed building was initially a house for the ferryman and his family. Over the years it has had many uses, including a farmhouse, while today it serves as a pub.

4 River Lea

The River Lea rises near Luton in Bedfordshire and flows for 68km before reaching the Thames at Bow Creek.

In 896, Alfred the Great ordered the level of the Lea to be lowered by digging a drainage canal to prevent the Danes invading Anglo-Saxon land by boat. Not only did this action deter the Danes, it also drained much of the marshland close to the river, making it more arable. This was a practice that continued well into the Middle Ages.

The river has powered many watermills for the grinding of locally grown cereals. These operated in abundance along the river banks until the advent of the steam engine. The watercourse has also been a vital supply of drinking water to the growing capital, while it also supplies water to the human-made stream, the New River. During the 9th century, the River Lea formed a frontier between the territories of the warring Anglo-Saxons and the Danes. It would later become the natural county boundary between London and Essex until local government reforms in the 1960s.

The eastern side of the Lea was beyond the control of the London County Council and so it was here that many of the 'stink industries' (the manufacturers of glue, rubber, gas, asbestos and chemicals) would base their factories once banished from London. In many places by the banks of the Lea, the land was prone to flooding, therefore cheap to acquire. The prevailing westerly winds would push the foul smells north-eastwards and away from the capital.

Lee or Lea? The name of the river can vary. Since 1571, all Acts of Parliament with reference to the river name it the *Lee*. Prior to this time, it was sometimes known as the *River Ley*. Today, most maps refer to the river as *Lea*, although Ordnance Survey Maps denote the river as both *Lea* and *Lee*. The recreation parks and authorities adjacent to the river tend to use the *Lee* option, i.e. Lee Valley Regional Park Authority, though the geographic area can be called *Lea*, e.g. Lower Lea Valley. The canalised version of the river is always the River *Lee* Navigation.

1 Walthamstow Wetlands

These urban wetlands, the largest in Europe, contain ten working reservoirs that cover 210ha and was opened to the public in 2017. The reservoirs are managed by Thames Water in partnership with London Borough of Waltham Forest and the London Wildlife Trust. The Marine Engine House pumping station, which pumped water from the Coppermill Stream into the reservoirs, is now the main visitor centre. The pumping station was built in 1894 (see *image page 63*) and remained in service until the 1980s. The chimney was removed once the pumps were converted to electric power and replaced with a Swift Tower, so called as it houses over 50 swift nest boxes and a roost for bats.

The Wetlands is a Site of Special Scientific Interest (SSSI). Among the birds that appear here are songbirds such as warblers, thrushes and finches. Several species of raptors can be viewed here, including kestrels, red kites, marsh harriers and sparrowhawks. Heron Island (**1a**) within reservoir No 5 contains about 40 nesting pairs of herons.

2 The Reservoirs

As the population of London trebled in the 60 years from 1801, the demand for clean, safe water increased. From 1863 until 1904 ten reservoirs were created in this area around the River Lea. Water from these reservoirs is piped through to the Stoke Newington reservoirs, 2km to the south-west (page 54). Today these water reserves supply 3.5 million Londoners. The reservoirs are also London's largest fishing area and it is possible to catch pike, trout, bream and carp.

3 Coppermill Tower

A small manufacturing facility was built here in 1806 to crush linseed into oil. But within a few years the site's usage had changed to processing copper. Copper ore was shipped in from Wales and transported up the River Lea by barge to be smelted and rolled into sheets. Production ceased in 1857 and the site was acquired by the East London Waterworks Company, which built a pumping station on the site. The Italianate tower was added in 1864 and is now a free-to-access observation platform.

4 Springfield Park

The recreation park was opened to the public in 1905. It was once the grounds of three private houses with gardens sloping down to the Lea. One of these was Springfield House, which was built around 1820 and from which the park took its name. The Grade II house, now known as the White Lodge Mansion, functions as the park's café. On the opposite

Below left: the Coppermill with its observation platform. Right: a cormorant flies over Walthamstow Marshes.

bank of the Lea is the Springfield Marina (**4a**), home to around a 100 pleasure crafts and barges.

5 Walthamstow Marshes Like many sections of land adjoining the River Lea, Walthamstow Marshes have, over the centuries, been drained and converted into arable land. These marshes were designated 'Lammas Land' where commoners could graze their animals once the harvest had been gathered in and before planting for the next season, typically between August and April. Local resistance fought off pressure to develop this wetland into industrial space and today it is part of the Lee Valley Regional Park Authority. The marshes are open spaces for walking and cycling.

A plaque on the railway arch commemorates the first flight.

2 The former 'bargee' school In the 19th century, entire families lived on barges as they moved materials and produce up and down the River Lee Navigation. Ensuring their children were educated could be difficult given their itinerant occupation. So, in 1841, this tiny building, resembling a chapel, was built as the St James Mission Room to educate the children of bargees as they were passing through. Today, it is the Chan Khong Monastery.

3 Nature's Throne This array of granite stones, created in 1990 by stone sculptor Paula Haughney, is also known as Hackney Henge. It is an arrangement of foundation blocks taken from the former engine house that stood on this site.

1 The first all-British powered flight Pioneering pilot and engineer Edwin Alliot Verdon Roe (1877–1958) made the first all-British powered flight on Walthamstow Marshes in 1909 (the Wright Brothers had carried out the world's first successful powered flight six years earlier). Roe rented two of the railway arches next to the River Lea to assemble his aircraft. The engines were manufactured in nearby Tottenham. It took him several attempts but eventually he managed to fly his *Roe I* triplane 300m in July that year. The following year, Roe, along with his businessman brother Humphrey Verdon Roe, established the company Avro Aircraft. During the First World War the company manufactured over 8,000 Avro 504 biplanes. Between the two world wars Roe lost control of his company and resigned. However, the name lived on through the design and development of the Avro Lancaster, Shackleton and Vulcan bombers.

4 Middlesex Filter Beds Nature Reserve Following a major outbreak of cholera in London in 1849, there developed a greater desire for cleaner water. The filter beds were established here three years later. After the plant closure in 1969, it was converted into a nature reserve and is home to over 200 species of plants. Kingfishers and grey wagtails can be spotted by the weir. Located within the reserve are many redundant parts of the former water treatment machinery and tanks.

5 Hackney Marshes This large expanse of former marshland is probably the spiritual home of Sunday league football. It contains 82 full size football pitches plus several rugby and cricket pitches with numerous changing rooms and facilities. During the 1980s, a young David Beckham started his footballing career here.

The land sits between the River Lee and the River Lee Navigation (or Hackney Cut). At 136ha it is one of the largest commons in Greater London. Prior to the land being purchased by the London County Council in 1893, it was prone to flooding and not at all suitable for domestic or industrial structures. An attempt to drain part of the marsh took place in 1757, during which a Roman causeway and coins were unearthed. The LCC completed the drainage programme and transformed it into the sports ground we see today. The perimeter of the sports field is lined with mainly lime and ash trees.

Clockwise from left: the triplane Roe1 flies over Walthamstow Marshes in 1909; football on the Hackney Marshes; Nature's Throne within the former Middlesex Filter Beds; former 'bargee' school.

1 The former Matchbox factory

Just before Homerton Road bridge, on the opposite bank, is a colourful, modern residential complex named Matchmakers Wharf. On this site once stood the Matchbox toy factory.

Lesney Products was formed in 1947, by Leslie Smith and Rodney Smith (not related) and so named by amalgamating their first names. They began by producing diecast components for industry. But they found real success by producing a replica of Queen Elizabeth's coronation coach in 1953. Lesney went on to produce further small toy vehicles that could be fit into a matchbox, with the packaging following suit.

By 1969, the factory was producing 1 million units a day and employing 3,600 people. However, the toys fell out of favour in the early 1980s, and with overseas competition mounting, the company went into liquidation in 1982. The factory was eventually demolished in 2010.

2 Here East

Once beyond the A12 dual carriageway the Queen Elizabeth Olympic Park begins to hove into view. Here East is a media centre that was created for the 2012 Olympic Games and built over a former Hackney Wick greyhound and speedway stadium. During the Games the facility accommodated over 20,000 international print and television journalists, crew and technical support staff. Following this, the building was repurposed and is now the broadcasting centre for BT Sport and a campus for several universities. The V&A East Storehouse, due to open in 2025, will act as a new accessible museum archive.

3 Queen Elizabeth Olympic Park

In 2005, London was awarded the rights to host the 2012 Olympic and Paralympic Games. The area just to the west of Stratford was chosen as the site to build five sports arenas, for track and field, swimming and diving, cycling and BMX racing and hockey, plus indoor sports arenas for basketball, volleyball and shooting. An athletes' village with over 17,000 beds was constructed nearby too. The plan was for all the facilities to be reused after the Games and that no 'white elephants' would remain. Improvements and upgrades were made to the local transport infrastructure including the Docklands Light Railway and the North London Line.

By the 20th century most of the 227ha of the Olympic park-to-be was either marshland with a few stink industries operating here, such as bone works, chemical plants, brewers, a fish smokery, a small oil refinery and even a small nuclear reactor. In 2007, a total of 280 businesses were operating on site and needed to be relocated. Some of the land had been contaminated and required cleaning. Many businesses had to be compulsory purchased by the Olympic Park developers. Fifty-two electricity pylons bestrode this area and these had to be taken down and the cables run underground. A series of water channels, the Bow Back Rivers, snaked through the zone, one of which, Pudding Mill River, had to be infilled in order to build the new Olympic stadium.

Once the Games had finished, work began to repurpose the stadia and park for future use (page 71). The entire area has since been transformed and has attracted new developments nearby, such as the huge Westfield Shopping Centre. Several institutions, including the V&A, the BBC and Sadler's Wells, are planning to develop outposts with the East Bank project. The park is now a large area of young trees, greenery, modern stadia, managed wetlands and waterways.

4 The Velodrome

As part of the 2012 Olympic and Paralympic Games a 6,000-capacity Velodrome with a 250m track was commissioned and built at the northern end of the Queen Elizabeth Olympic Park. It was the first of the London Olympic stadiums to be completed, opening in 2011. Adjacent to the Velodrome, an outdoor BMX track and an 8km mountain bike trail were also created for the Games and built over the former Eastway Cycle Circuit. The new cycling arena earned the nickname 'The Pringle' due to its wave-

Above: the Olympic rings and the Velodrome, part of the Lee Valley VeloPark. Below left: the Here East logo above the media centre.

shaped roof. GB Cycling had enormous success at the venue, winning seven gold medals out of a possible ten. The Velodrome and the Lee Valley VeloPark continues to host national and international cycle and BMX events.

Walking these pages 2.1km

3 East Bank

3 East Bank East Bank is a massive new education and cultural complex just to the north-west of the Aquatics Centre. When complete it will provide new studios, theatre and recording facilities for the BBC, which is moving its famous Maida Vale Studio to the Queen Elizabeth Olympic Park. It will also provide a new home for the BBC Symphony Orchestra and BBC Singers and it is due to open in 2025.

The internationally renowned dance organisation Sadler's Wells is also creating a flexible theatre space here for an extensive variety of dance performances, while the UAL London College of Fashion has already relocated its multi-site facilities into a campus at East Bank. The V&A East Museum is also planning a new exhibition space here, which will open in 2025.

1 London Blossom Garden This garden is a memorial to all those who lost their lives during the Covid-19 pandemic and the key workers who kept the hospitals and the capital running during the crisis. With 33 trees, one for each borough of London and the City of London, it is a place of refuge and quiet contemplation. The spring blossoming trees include hawthorn, cherry plum and other cherry varieties and are sited within a secluded and embanked section of the park.

2 Wetland Walk Part of the London Organising Committee of the Olympic and Paralympic Games (LOCOG) remit was to clean and restore much of the former industrial landscape it had acquired. On the eastern banks of the River Lea, north of the Olympic Stadium, a wetland area with several ponds has been created with walkways that run through and around it. These wetlands also act as a flood defence; in the case of extremely heavy rainfall and the rise of the Lea's water levels, water is allowed to flow into this area to protect nearby housing.

Thousands of wetland plants have been introduced here, including reeds, sedges, grasses and wet wildflowers, which attract a range of birds and wildlife.

4 London Stadium Formerly known as the Olympic Stadium, this arena was specifically created to host the track and field events at the London Olympic and Paralympic Games in 2012, plus the opening and closing ceremonies. It was built on an island within the complex of the Bow Back Rivers with one of the streams, Pudding Mill River, being infilled in 2007 to make way for the stadium. Part of the brief for the architects Populous was that the arena should be not become redundant once the games had finished but should be resized and repurposed for other sports.

During the games' athletics events, Team GB won four Olympic gold medals (including two for Sir Mo Farah in the 5,000m and 10,000m events) and 11 Paralympics gold medals.

West Ham FC later negotiated a deal to lease the stadium and in 2016 the team began playing Premier League football here, once the capacity had been reduced from 80,000 to 60,000. The arena, renamed London Stadium, is also used for concerts, athletics, baseball, rugby league and rugby union games.

5 London Aquatics Centre Designed by architect Zaha Hadid, this 160m parabolic-arched structure represents 'the fluid geometry of water in motion'. Of all the 2012 Olympic stadia, with its two 50m pools and a 24m diving pool, this is probably the most stunning and elegant. In the Paralympic Games, Ellie Simmonds won two gold medals here and set a World Record in the 400m freestyle.

During the Olympic and Paralympic Games this arena seated 17,500 people through the use of two temporary wings attached to the structure. These were removed after the Games to reveal the true dynamics of the centre. Once repurposed the facility, with a capacity of 2,800, opened to all in 2014 for swimming, diving and competitions.

Clockwise from top left: London Aquatics Centre; a view of London Stadium and the River Lea from the Eastcross Bridge; the Wetland Walk.

1 ArcelorMittal Orbit This radical, quirky and controversial sculptural observation tower was conceived by artist Anish Kapoor and engineer Cecil Balmond in response to a competition to create a focal point for the Olympic Park. The steel magnate Lakshmi Mittal contributed £16 million towards the £19 million project, and the tower was constructed from 60 per cent recycled steel produced by an ArcelorMittal factory in Luxembourg.

The ArcelorMittal Orbit is now the UK's tallest piece of public art. However, the red looping structure and fluid design received many negative reviews from critics questioning the need for such a 'pointless, inelegant tower'. However, at 115m high, the Orbit's two viewing platforms offer an impressive view of the Olympic Park and the London vista beyond. In 2016, the world's longest slide, at 178m, was added to the structure.

2 The Greenway Beneath this footpath are several large, cast-iron pipes that carry 455 million litres of sewage daily to the Beckton Treatment Works 7km to the east. The pipes are known as the Northern Outfall Sewer and were constructed in 1861 as part of the London sewage network established by the Metropolitan Board of Works and its chief engineer Sir Joseph Bazalgette. During the 1850s, several outbreaks of cholera and the 'Great Stink' of 1858 prompted the government to act and prevent raw sewage being discharged into the Thames and its tributaries.

A footpath and cycleway, named The Greenway, was constructed in the 1990s, above the interceptor sewage pipes. It runs from Wick Lane, just to the west of the Queen Elizabeth Olympic Park to Beckton, and forms part of the Capital Ring Walk.

3 Olympic Torch sculpture This Ikea-sponsored lattice sculpture of wood and steel stands 40m tall and was constructed in 2012 to coincide with the Games.

4 Abbey Mills Pumping Station This shiny aluminium building, visible across the Prescott Channel, is a modern sewage pumping station, which replaced the brick structure to its left in 1997. The 19th-century pumping station on Abbey Lane was built in 1868 to pump effluent in the Northern Outfall Sewer and then on to Beckton Treatment Works. It formed part of Sir Joseph Bazalgette's master plan to improve the sewage disposal system within the capital. The Abbey Mills Pumping Station gained its name from a water mill that once stood upon this site within the grounds of the former Stratford Langthorne Abbey.

Designed by the architect Charles Driver, the structure has been described as a 'cathedral of sewage' owing to its Venetian gothic appearance. Most of the new Victorian sewage system was buried below ground and invisible. So, when the opportunity arose to build a feature above the surface, much was made of the details and ready money lavished upon it. Originally the station had two Byzantine-style chimneys adjacent to the site, but these were removed during the Second World War as they might have been used for navigation by Luftwaffe pilots. The eight steam engine pumps were withdrawn in the 1930s and replaced with electric motors. The Abbey Mills Pumping Station is still used today if demand is high.

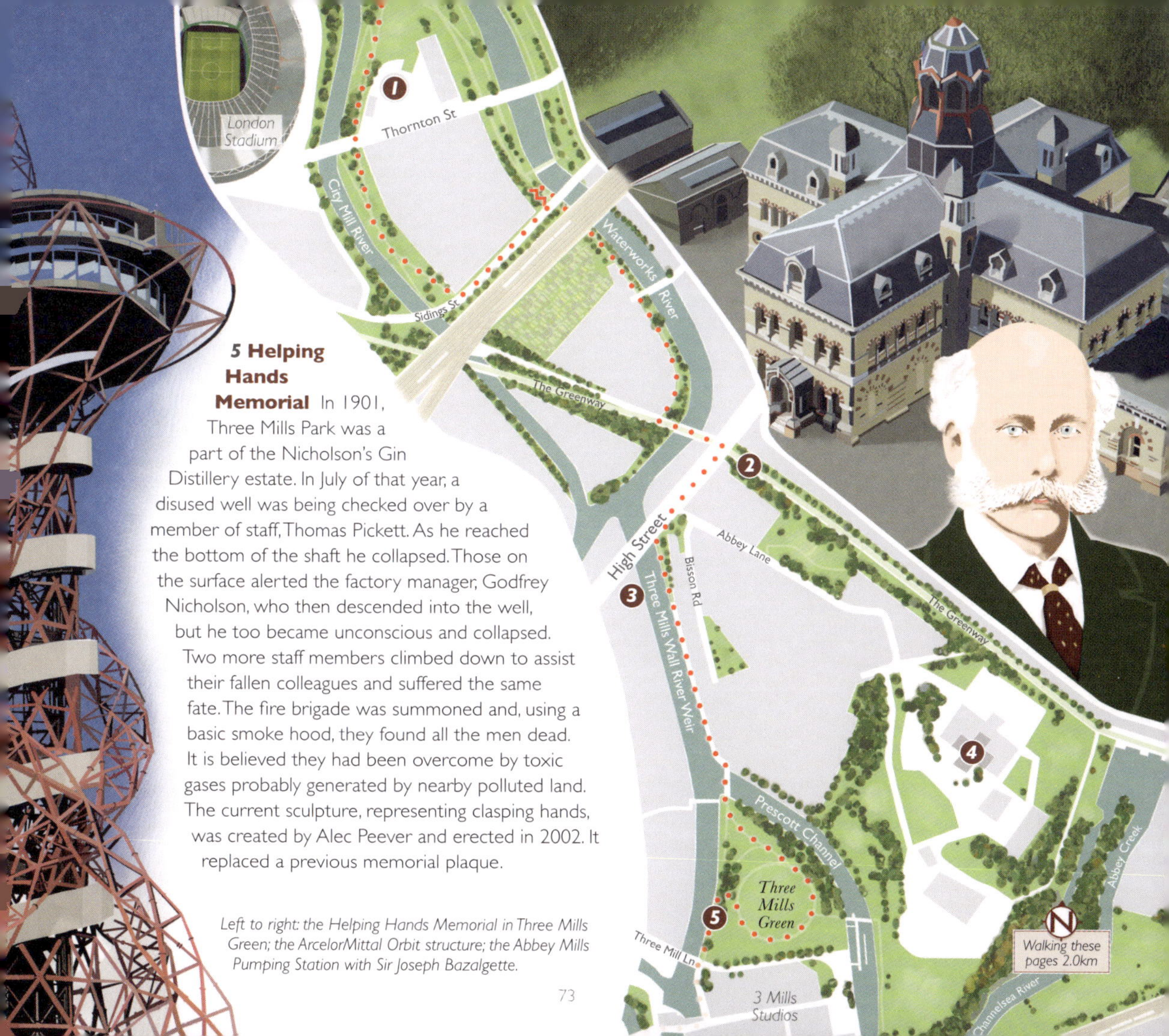

5 Helping Hands Memorial

In 1901, Three Mills Park was a part of the Nicholson's Gin Distillery estate. In July of that year, a disused well was being checked over by a member of staff, Thomas Pickett. As he reached the bottom of the shaft he collapsed. Those on the surface alerted the factory manager, Godfrey Nicholson, who then descended into the well, but he too became unconscious and collapsed. Two more staff members climbed down to assist their fallen colleagues and suffered the same fate. The fire brigade was summoned and, using a basic smoke hood, they found all the men dead. It is believed they had been overcome by toxic gases probably generated by nearby polluted land. The current sculpture, representing clasping hands, was created by Alec Peever and erected in 2002. It replaced a previous memorial plaque.

Left to right: the Helping Hands Memorial in Three Mills Green; the ArcelorMittal Orbit structure; the Abbey Mills Pumping Station with Sir Joseph Bazalgette.

1 3 Mills Studios The Nicholson family began distilling gin in London in 1736. In 1872, they moved production to the Three Mills Distillery. During a German bombing raid in 1941, part of the distillery was destroyed and the plant closed permanently.

In the 1990s, several television and film production companies created studio spaces on Three Mills Island. The London Development Agency, in 2004, leased the 3 Mills Studios to encourage and support these creative businesses. The studios now offer over 7ha of filming, television and rehearsal space.

Films such as *28 Days Later*, *Never Let Me Go*, and *Lock, Stock and Two Smoking Barrels* were filmed here. The television series *MasterChef* and *RuPaul's Drag Race UK* were also produced at 3 Mills, while many major British theatre and dance companies use the rehearsal facilities, including English National Opera, Matthew Bourne's New Adventures and English National Ballet.

2 The House and Clock Mills The tranquil and bucolic location of Three Mills Island is quite unique given its closeness to the centre of London. Water-powered tidal mills have operated here since the Stratford Langthorne Abbey was founded nearly 900 years ago. In 1727, the medieval tidal mill was bought by three Huguenots for the propose of grinding flour.

The House Mill (**2a**) was constructed here in 1776, by Daniel Bisson. It is the largest tidal mill in the world, though currently not operating. Water from the incoming tide was stored in a pond behind the Mill. As the tide turned, the sluice gates were opened to drive the four paddle wheels. These in turn would power 12 pairs of mill stones. The House Mill is now a Grade I listed building and is open to visitors on Sundays from the beginning of April until early December. The charitable trust that runs the mill is hoping to start generating hydro-electricity by installing three turbines in place of the mill wheels.

The Clock Mill (**2b**) was added to the site in 1817 to grind flour but later became involved in the production of gin. The oast towers were added to dry hops. The Clock Mill continued operating until 1952.

Grey wagtails, herons and common sandpipers can often be seen flying around the tidal stream and mudflats.

3 Bromley-By-Bow Gasworks The Imperial Gas Light and Coke Company began construction of nine gas holders in

1870 with the gasworks located to the south.
In 1817, this had been the site of an East India
Company factory used in the production of Congreve
rockets. During the Anglo-Mysore Wars, the British army had
come under attack from enemy rockets, and William Congreve,
military officer and inventor, was commissioned to create a military
rocket that would be more effective than the enemy's in the field of battle.
The gas holders are still in place, though gas production ceased in the early
1960s.

4 Bow Locks and Creek The walk continues southwards along a sliver
of land (or isthmus) that divides the River Lee Navigation and the Channelsea
River. Weir. Depending upon the tide, the heights of the two streams can vary
considerably. Once the two are united after the Bow Locks it becomes the
Bow Creek, which then meanders for nearly 4km until it reaches the
Thames. Visible from the Bow Lock footbridge is the Limehouse
Cut. This canal was created in 1770 so that boats and barges
heading to the London Docks could
avoid the long Thames loop around
the Isle of Dogs.

Left: the House and Clock Mills.

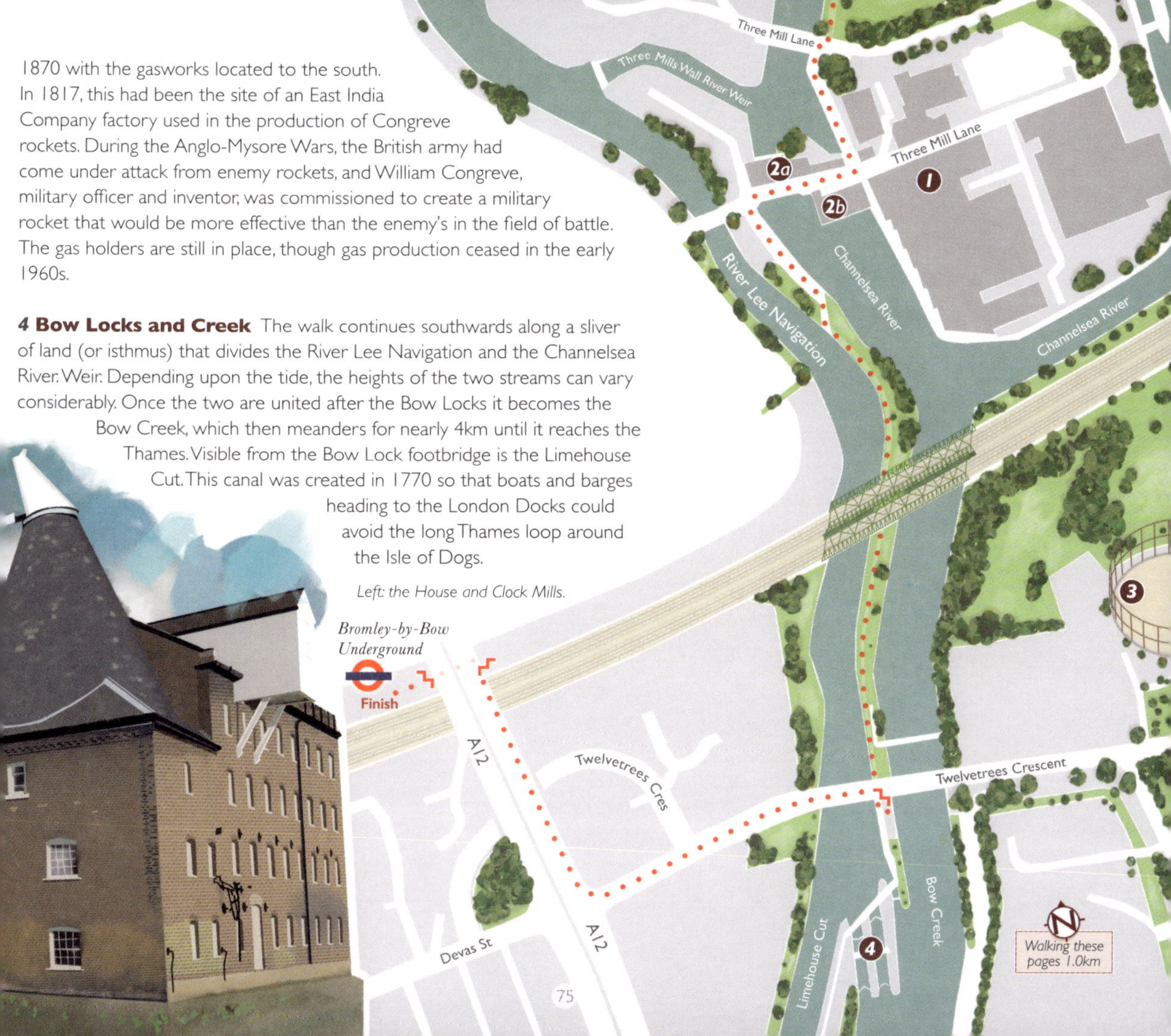

Opposite: Regent´s Canal adjacent to Victoria Park.

LONDON FIELDS – TOWER HAMLETS CEMETERY PARK

The East End of London was once a heavily industrialised area with factories and workshops belching out great volumes of toxic smoke. Today, it is much improved and is a great place for a green walk.

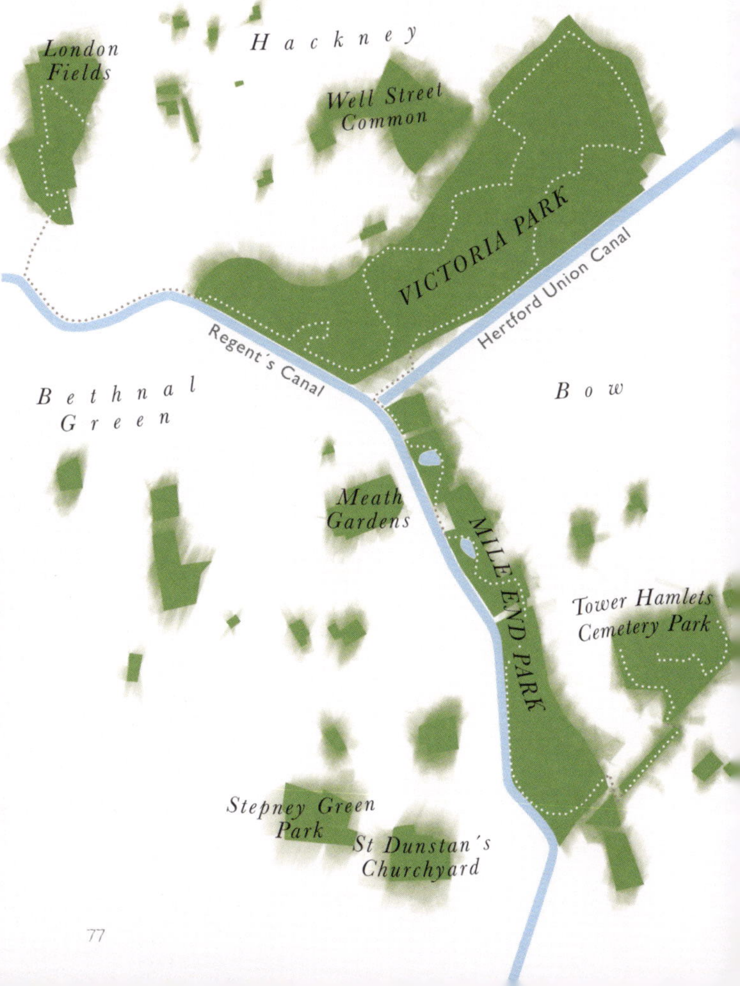

LONDON FIELDS – TOWER HAMLETS CEMETERY PARK

Total walking distance 11.6km

This is a relatively flat walk along a now fashionable East End market street, around the largest municipal and most popular park in London. The route continues along a canal that was once a super highway of its day and whose banks have been transformed with cultural pavilions and a dedicated green bridge for walkers and cyclists. The walk concludes in one of London's 'Magnificent Seven' cemeteries.

1 London Fields This 12.5ha section of common land was once used by drovers to hold cattle and sheep in pens overnight as they headed into and out of the capital's markets. Until the early 19th century London Fields was surrounded by orchards and farmland. It was also reported that highwaymen frequented this area.

Today, London Fields contains a cricket pitch, a 50m lido, tennis courts, children's play areas and a wildflower meadow. The first recorded game of cricket played here was in September 1802, between two teams: London Fields and their neighbours, Clapton (Clapton won by an innings and 49 runs).

During the Second World War, parts of the East End were destroyed by enemy bombing. Housing was in short supply and to help alleviate the problem the government began a programme of creating prefabricated housing. Eighteen of these temporary structures were located on London Fields, just to the south of the lido. They are no longer standing.

2 London Fields Lido The outdoor pool was created in 1932 by the London County Council and comprised of separate male and female pools. These were later united to create one 50m pool. The lido closed in 1988 due to funding cuts. However, after a popular and lengthy campaign to restore the pool, the lido finally reopened in 2007.

3 The *Flower Sellers* This mosaic-covered sculpture was created in the late 1980s, and is known as the *Flower Sellers*. The sculpted sheep surrounding the main figures commemorate that London Fields was used for grazing livestock several centuries ago.

4 Broadway Market This street, once named Porter's Path, was an historic highway vital for the transportation of food and animals into the City of London and the Docks.

The cattle drovers have long gone and now around 70 shops line the Broadway, selling everything from healing crystals and vintage clothing to ethically sourced coffees and fine wines. Each Saturday sees a thriving street market selling fresh food and produce, plus plenty of street food offerings.

Clockwise from left: the mosaic-covered sculpture, The Flower Sellers; the wildflower meadow on London Fields; the fascia of the former eel and pie shop F Cooke on Broadway Market.

5 F Cooke – eel and pie house In 1900, Frederick Cooke opened an eel and pie house at 9 Broadway Market, renowned for its pie and mash and jellied eels. The business started in 1862, when Robert Cooke, Frederick's father, opened a shop near Brick Lane, east London, selling stewed eels and pies. It became a huge success, so he and his family opened more outlets in other parts of the capital, including in Stratford, Dalston and Bermondsey.

In late 2020, during the Covid-19 pandemic, the owner, Bob Cooke (great grandson of Robert), decided to close down the shop in Broadway Market. The shop's interior and exterior are Grade II listed, meaning the new retailers retained the fascia at the expense of their own branding. The Cooke family have now moved to Essex and established their famous eel and pie houses in Chelmsford and Romford.

1 Bethnal Green Gasholders These two empty gas holders have towered over the Regent's Canal for many years. The gas storage containers were once connected to the adjacent Imperial Gas Works in Haggerston. The canal enabled coal to be shipped easily into the works for processing into town gas. Planning permission has been granted to build circular blocks of residential apartments within the structures.

2 Regent's Canal A hundred years ago this quiet waterway was teeming with barges carrying everything from pig-iron and pianos to crockery and compost. In the late 1960s, the canal fell into decline and today its use is being redefined.

A period known as 'canal mania' had begun in 1761, when the Duke of Bridgewater had a human-made waterway constructed to transport coal from his mines in Worsley to Manchester and parts of the north-west of England. Transportation by barge was slow but huge amounts of heavy goods could be shipped safely and cheaply by water. London was a relative latecomer to the canal revolution. In 1801, the Grand Junction Canal (now the Grand Union Canal) finally reached Paddington in west London. At about this time, the inland West India Docks opened in the Isle of Dogs, to the east of the capital. Yet raw materials and finished goods still had to be transported by horse and wagon between the two points and the need for a canal linking Paddington and the Thames was becoming very apparent.

In 1810, the Regent's Canal Company was formed and digging of the waterway commenced two years later. The architect and visionary John Nash became a director of the company. Nash had plans to run the canal through the new Regent's Park as a water feature, though this never came to fruition. Regent's Canal finally opened in 1820. At the time of its opening, the waterway ran through open countryside and farmland. Very quickly, the expanding capital enveloped the canal and places such as Camden grew on the business that the canal brought. Several gasworks were established on the banks of the waterway as coal could be efficiently shipped in. Regent's Canal continued to operate as a commercial route until 1969, when after succumbing to competition from motor vehicles, it closed and fell into decline.

Over the past 40 years the once grimy canal and its towpaths have seen a revival and renovation. Once inhospitable, it is now home to fashionable waterside apartments and restaurants. Places such as Camden and King's Cross have also seen massive makeovers. The towpath is now a very beneficial foot and cycleway connecting north London to the Thames in the east.

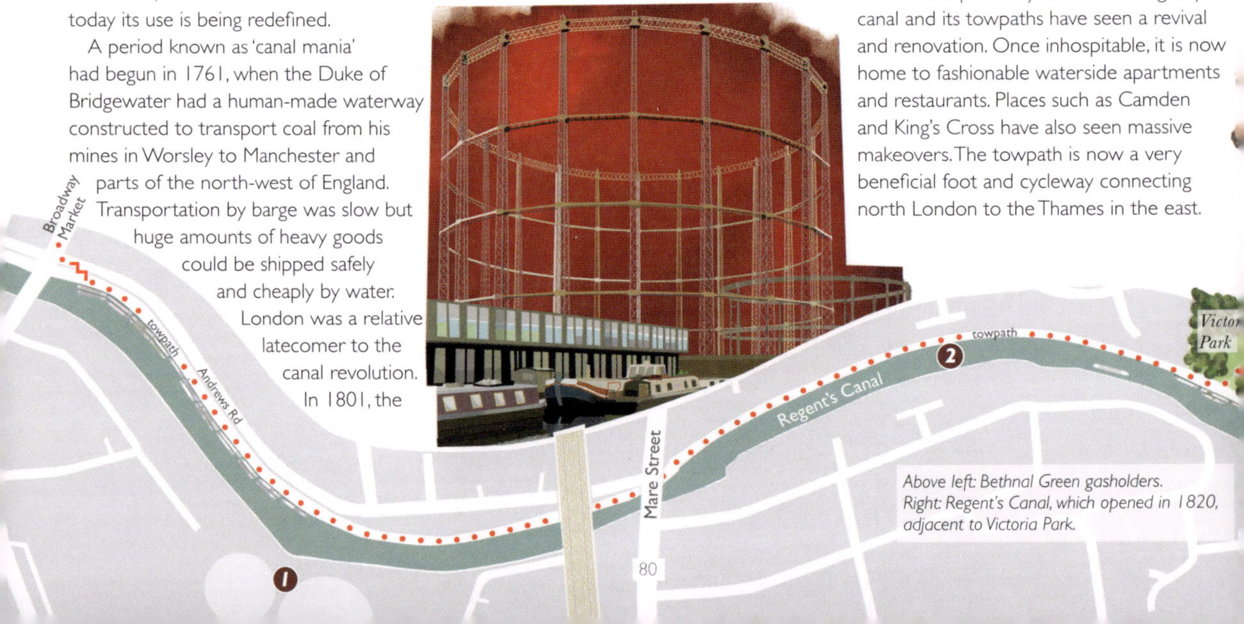

Above left: Bethnal Green gasholders.
Right: Regent's Canal, which opened in 1820, adjacent to Victoria Park.

N
Walking these
pages 0.8km

1 Victoria Park By the 1830s, much of the East End of London was a squalid expanse of poor housing interspersed by factories with chimneys belching noxious and dangerous odours into the atmosphere. Life expectancy here was short and the locals had fewer places to avoid the stink as more factories and houses were being built.

Around this time, a petition with 30,000 signatures was raised and presented to Queen Victoria for the creation of a new protected park in the East End for locals to enjoy and escape the rigours of daily life. Money was raised from the sale of a property belonging to the late Duke of York. The former estate of the heretic-burning Bishop Bonner (1500–1569) was purchased and the architect Sir James Pennethorne (1801–1871) was appointed as the landscape designer. Pennethorne, a relative of John Nash, would later go on to design Battersea and Kennington Parks.

Victoria Park opened in 1845 and at 86ha it is the largest municipal park in the capital. Shaped like a giant Wellington boot, it is bordered on two sides by the Regent's and Hertford Union Canals. This much-loved and popular 'People's Park' soon became a big attraction for local inhabitants, including being a gathering spot for political rallies for groups such as the Chartists and the Suffragettes. Many influential speakers addressed meetings here, including George Bernard Shaw,

Annie Besant, Ben Tillett and William Morris (page 122).

In 1900, the park contained 32 cricket pitches and 37 tennis courts. During the 1930s, Fred Perry, winner of three Wimbledon Championships, would practice here.

During the Second World War the park was partially closed so that anti-aircraft guns could be installed to protect the East End from German bombers. This made the park a target for attack and several features, including a church and an arcade shelter designed by Pennethorne, were destroyed.

Since the late 1970s, the park has been used as a large music venue. In 1978, the first Rock Against Racism concert was held here. Today, it hosts the popular All Points East festival each May. These events raise money essential for the maintenance of the park. With its numerous sports facilities and lakes, the park now attracts around 9 million visitors per year and is regularly voted the most popular park in the UK.

2 The Dogs of Alcibiades The dog statues located at Bonner Gate are based on a 2nd century BC Greek sculpture of a Molossian hound, a muscular and aggressive guard dog. The breed is now extinct. The original sculpture was looted by the Romans in 168 BC. Around 1755, Henry Jennings bought the stone sculpture in Rome

and shipped it to London. Over the years many copies of the dog have been made and it became fashionable to display dog sculptures on country estates. A pair of dogs were presented to Victoria Park in 1912 by a benefactor, Lady Regnart. Within a hundred years, the dogs had been so vandalised and weathered that they had to be replaced and located behind railings.

The original Greek sculpture, the Jennings Dog, is today on display in the British Museum.

3 The Pagoda In 1842, Chinese Summerhouse was created for an exhibition on China in Hyde Park. Following the exposition, the structure was dismantled and rebuilt in newly opened Victoria Park and renamed the Pagoda. During the Second World War the Pagoda was badly damaged during a bombing raid and was finally demolished in 1956.

In 2012, a replacement was created on a human-made island within the West Lake. The pagoda is accessible over two footbridges.

Far left: the Chinese Pagoda. Left: the Dogs of Alcibiades at Bonner Gate.

1 Baroness Burdett-Coutts Drinking Fountain The Victorian philanthropist Baroness Angela Burdett-Coutts (1814–1906) was the richest woman in Britain during the late Victorian era. She donated this lavish gothic drinking fountain in 1862, to provide visitors to the park with safe, clean drinking water. In 1975, the fountain was granted Grade II status and as part of the London 2012 Olympic Games refurbishment, it underwent a restoration. Sadly, the drinking water facility was not repaired to working order. Given the tons of plastic bottles that must be discarded in the park each year, this does seem erroneous.

2 The East Lake In 1875, this lake was created as a bathing facility for men and it remained as such until just before the Second World War. Most Victorian working-class houses possessed little or no washing facilities and a dip in these ponds was the only way people could get clean. At the beginning of the 20th century a separate lake was created exclusively for women bathers. In 1936, a lido was opened near to Grove Road, but it closed in 1976 and the buildings were demolished in 1990, despite public outcry. A car park now covers the site. The East Lake is now popular with anglers, and fish such as tench, gudgeon, chub and roach can be caught. This lake and other water features within Victoria Park have attracted many species of water birds, including grey herons, mute swans, kingfishers, coots, moorhens and cormorants.

3 The Old English Gardens These symmetrically laid-out gardens were planted in 1916 with rose beds, topiary and border plants. It is a colourful oasis within the greenery of Victoria Park. There is an abundance of seating to allow people to relax and take in the vista.

4 The former St Augustine's Church A small, plaqueless memorial stone is located just off the footpath and marks where the altar of St Augustine's Church once stood. This place of worship was constructed in 1867 within the park to accommodate the religious needs of the expanding population of the East End of London. A line of lime trees marks where the north-west and south-west church walls

5 London Bridge Stone Alcoves

When many of the old houses were removed from London Bridge in 1758, 14 stone shelters were built to protect pedestrians from the wind and rain. These were commissioned by the owners of the crossing, Bridge House Estates. By the turn of the 19th century the bridge was well past its usefulness: it was too narrow and was sinking into the Thames. A new London Bridge was built 30m to the west and, once completed, the old bridge was dismantled and the stone shelters were placed in storage. In 1860, two of the alcoves were reconstructed here in the northern section of the park.

once stood. St Augustine's was damaged by bombing during the Second World War and demolished soon afterwards.

Trees in the park

There are around 4,500 trees in Victoria Park. These include many of the standard British trees such as oaks, maples, limes, horse chestnuts and London planes. However, there are more exotic trees to be found including Persian Ironwood, gingko, cockspur and mulberry.

From far left: leaves of a lime tree; the Burdett-Coutts Drinking Fountain; a water nymph detail from the fountain; one of the two London Bridge stone alcoves with the Bridge House Estates insignia (located in the roof of the shelter); the former St Augustine's Church once sited within Victoria Park.

1 Victoria Park Raemers Skatepark

Named after the professional British skateboarder, Ben Raemers (1990–2019), this skatepark possesses a 'full cradle' or 3.6m bowl and is one of only two in the UK. It also features a number of ledges and a pump bump.

2 Hertford Union Canal

After 1820, horse-drawn barges travelling down the Lee Navigation (page 62) and wishing to access the newly opened Regent's Canal had a long journey down the Lee to the Limehouse Cut, River Thames* and finally into the Regent's Canal Basin in Limehouse; a journey of 8km.

Sir George Duckett, owner of the Stort Navigation (an off-shoot of the River Lee Navigation), saw the potential of creating a 2km waterway connecting the two canals (see map right). His plan was put in to action and in 1831 the Hertford Union Canal opened. However, the toll charges were high, which deterred many barge owners from using the new channel, and Duckett was declared bankrupt the following year. The Regent's Canal Company eventually took over the running of the canal.

The Limehouse Cut then fed into the Thames and not the Regent's Canal Basin.

3 Lakeview Estate

These two striking geometric-patterned 11-storey blocks of flats were designed by the Modernist architect Berthold Lubetkin in 1958. He is famous for his use of precast concrete sections and complex geometric designs. The blocks sit tightly between Old Ford Road and the canal. Lubetkin is probably best known for his design of the penguin pool in London Zoo, Regent's Park (page 41).

4 Mile End Park

During the German bombing raids of the Second World War many key areas of the East End were destroyed. The Regent's Canal was one such target as it connected the Docks to other parts of London and beyond. Following the war, this strip of land, 1.8km long and adjacent to the canal, was cleared of damaged houses and factories. A plan to create a green corridor was conceived during the war but not implemented until 1995. The now continuous, uninterrupted foot-and-cycle path from Victoria Park to Mile End Stadium was completed in 2002.

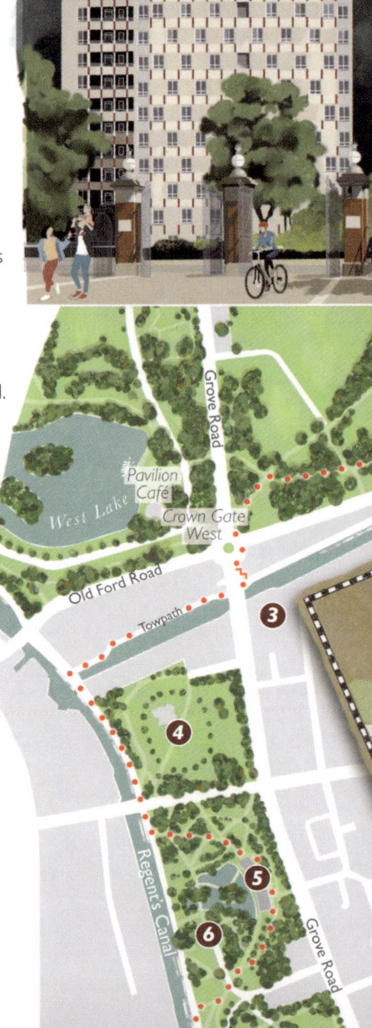

Alternative Routes

8km

2km

5 The Ecology Pavilion

The pavilion is an energy-efficient, earth-sheltered building with one of the heating inputs coming from sunlight radiating through the large double-glazed windows. Electricity is also gathered from a wind turbine. Rainwater is collected and repurposed within the structure. The pavilion, with its exposed timber posts, overlooks a series of lakes that are home to water birds, amphibians and some rare orchids. The building is used for functions and events.

6 The Palm Tree pub

This isolated 'East End boozer' is devoid of many 21st century facilities (e.g. it only takes cash). It stands alone in the grounds of the Ecology Pavilion and was originally built for Truman's Brewery in 1935. The building is now Grade II listed and was once a traditional street corner pub where two former streets once intersected until a German V2 rocket hit the neighbourhood. It now stands very much alone.

Clockwise from left: the Ecology Pavilion by Regent´s Canal; the Lakeview Estate viewed from Crown Gate West; a skateboarder at the Victoria Park Raemers Skatepark; a map of the East London waterways circa 1820.

Walking these pages 2.2km

1 The Art Pavilion The design and ethos of this Art Pavilion are very similar to its neighbour, the Ecology Pavilion to the north. It is also buried within a grass bank. A large, airy community gallery overlooks an elliptical-shaped lake and is managed by the London Borough of Tower Hamlets. The space is used for exhibitions, events and weddings.

2 The Art Mound This human-made hillock, with its spiral path, was created with spoil from local excavations. Part of these grounds were originally within the New Globe Tavern Gardens. The tavern, in the 1840s, stood on the corner of Mile End Road and the Regent's Canal and formed a recreational area for dancing, music and fireworks. Good views can be seen from the top of the mound.

3 The Green Bridge To connect the north section of the Mile End Park with the southern section, a 25m yellow foot-and-cycle bridge was constructed over Mile End Road. It was designed by Piers Gough of CZWG Architects and it opened to the public in 1999. Despite being planted with drought-resistant shrubs, on each of my visits to the bridge over the years they've always looked sad and in need of watering. However, the trees planted either side of the bridge are thriving. Its official name is the Green Bridge, but it is referred to locally as the 'Banana Bridge' because of its colouring and curvature.

Clockwise from left: the Ragged School Museum; the Art Pavilion; a Millenium National Cycle Network finger post (**4**); the Green Bridge (or Banana Bridge) reaching over Mile End Road.

5 The Ragged School Museum

When Thomas Barnardo arrived in London in 1866 to take up his medical training at the London Hospital in the East End, he soon became very aware of many children were sleeping rough and begging on the streets. Barnardo was born in Dublin in 1845 to a Jewish father and Irish mother. He had plans, after medical school, to become a missionary in China but he never completed his training. Appalled by what he had seen in the East End, he began his missionary work here and started raising funds for his first children's home. This was built a few hundred metres away from this spot in 1867. Ten years later, with the assistance of the social reformer Lord Shaftesbury, he established a 'Ragged School', in a warehouse on the bank of the Regent's Canal, where pupils were fed and given skills useful for a working life. The school's intake grew to 1,000 pupils and it became the largest in London. The building now houses a museum of Victorian school life, which opened in 1990 (an entry fee is charged).

6 Ackroyd Drive Green Link

These four small, urban chalk meadows (plus an allotment) were transformed in the 1990s, from an industrial wasteland into a green corridor to link up Mile End Park and Tower Hamlets Cemetery Park. They are bounded by a railway viaduct to the north, and a road and block of flats to the south.

Tower Hamlets Cemetery Park

This was the last of the 'Magnificent Seven' cemeteries to be created. Abney Park Cemetery (page 59) had been established in 1840, and the 1841 Act of Parliament enabled Tower Hamlets Cemetery to be created by a private company, which purchased 11ha of land south of Mile End Road. It was consecrated in the same year and within 50 years nearly a quarter of a million bodies were interred here. It became known locally as Bow Cemetery. Some of the public (paupers) graves contained up to 30 coffins in one plot alone.

During the Second World War, the Anglican and Byzantine-inspired chapels were both damaged by bombing and were later pulled down and the debris cleared. The cemetery was bombed five times during the war. By the time it closed in 1966, it contained 350,000 bodies. Following the closure, the GLC began to exhume thousands of bodies and these were reinterred in graves further away from London. In several parts of the cemetery today there are no visible tombstones.

In 1986, it was designated a local nature reserve and is now managed by the Friends of Tower Hamlets Cemetery Park. According to the Forestry Commission it is the most urban woodland in London, while it is a site of Metropolitan Importance for Nature Conservation.

Trees and wildlife within Cemetery Park

Tower Hamlets Cemetery Park is no longer a graveyard but a managed woodland where trees are encouraged to grow. On the southern edge of the park is a row of limes believed to be 300 years old (George II was on the throne). These are older than the cemetery itself and from a time when the area was countryside. Other trees to be found among the 47,000 head-stones include ash and sycamore.

The park is a sanctuary for up to 30 bird species, notable among these include sparrowhawk, chiffchaff, blackcap, green and great spotted woodpecker, plus the occasional common whitethroat and song thrush. Several pipistrelle bats species, grey squirrels and red foxes can also be observed here.

Burials

Many of the 'Magnificent Seven' cemeteries can claim famous Victorians interred within their graveyards: Highgate has philosopher and political theorist Karl Marx, while Kensal Green has the engineer Isambard Kingdom Brunel. Tower Hamlets Cemetery can't make such lofty declarations, but it can claim many lesser known but notable people of the 19th century.

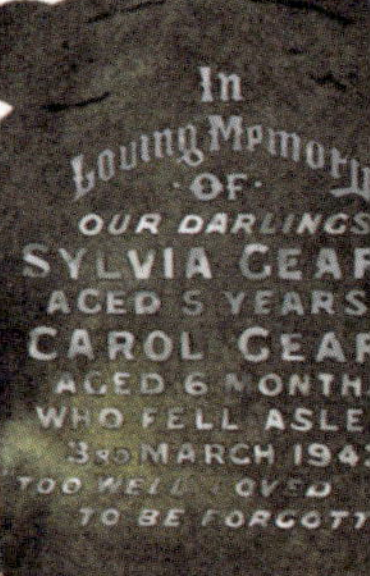

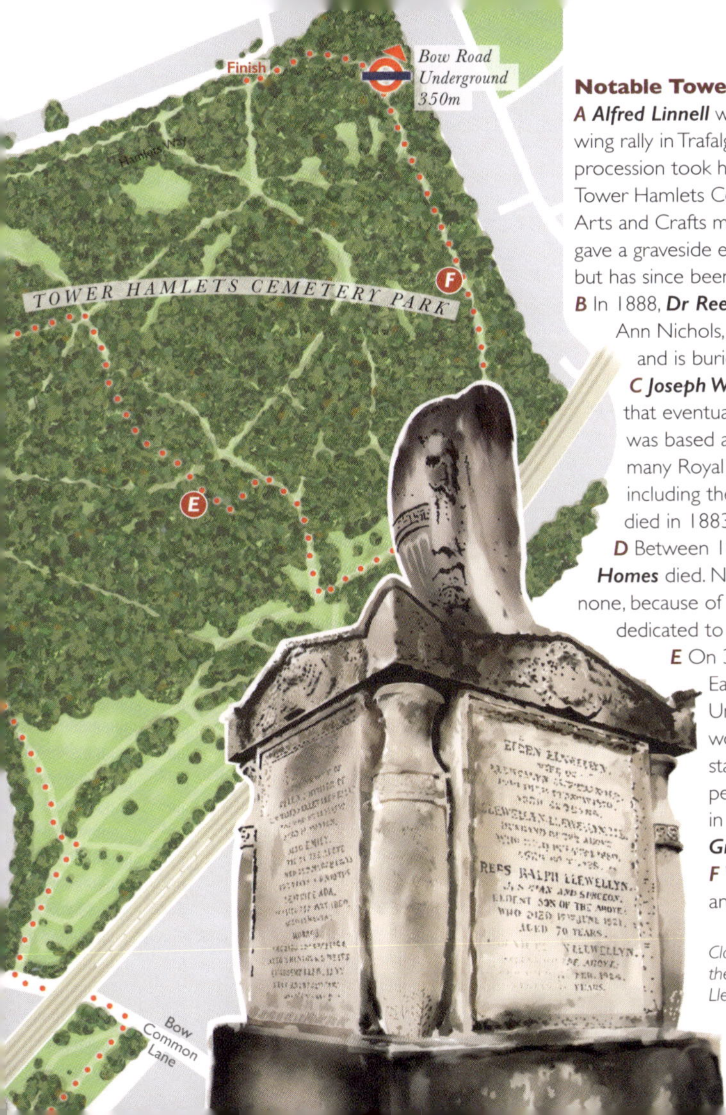

London Fields – Tower Hamlets Cemetery Park

Notable Tower Hamlets Cemetery graves

A *Alfred Linnell* was trampled by a police horse in 1887 during a left-wing rally in Trafalgar Square. He later died of his injuries. His funeral procession took hours to progress from its starting point in Soho to Tower Hamlets Cemetery. William Morris, socialist and leader of the Arts and Crafts movement (page 122), walked alongside the hearse and gave a graveside eulogy. The original grave was located near this spot, but has since been replaced by a modern tombstone.

B In 1888, **Dr Rees Ralph Llewellyn** performed an autopsy on Mary Ann Nichols, Jack the Ripper's first victim. He died in 1921, aged 70 and is buried here in the family grave.

C *Joseph Westwood* was the founder of a shipbuilding company that eventually became known as the Thames Iron Works and was based at Bow Creek. The company went on to construct many Royal Navy ships, including HMS *Warrior*, and bridges, including the one over the Thames at Westminster. Westwood died in 1883.

D Between 1876 and 1924 around 500 children of **Dr Barnardo's Homes** died. Nearly all of them were buried in this cemetery though none, because of cost, were given a headstone. A memorial stone dedicated to these children was erected here in 2016.

E On 3 March 1943, during a German air raid on the East End, many people rushed into Bethnal Green Underground Station, an air raid shelter, for safety. A woman and a child stumbled on the stairs and in the stampede many people fell over them. A total of 173 people, mainly women and children, died of asphyxiation in the crush. A number of the victims of **the Bethnal Green Tube Disaster** are buried at this location.

F *Will Crooks* leader of the 1889 London Dock Strike and first Labour mayor of Poplar. He died in 1921.

Clockwise from left: the Westwood Monument with the Dr Barnardo's memorial in the foreground; the Llewellyn family memorial; the grave of the Geary sisters, who died in the Bethnal Green Tube Disaster 1943.

Walking these pages 1.4km

Opposite: the Old Royal Naval Hospital with Queen's House and Greenwich Park in the distance.

SOUTH EAST LONDON

BLACKHEATH – MILLWALL DOCK

This walk starts at a place where armies and rebels once gathered, on through royal parkland with tremendous panoramic views of London and then to a city farm and former inland docks.

BLACKHEATH – MILLWALL DOCK

Total walking distance 8.3km

This is a fascinating walk of many contrasts, that descends from Blackheath, a former strategic location, into Royal Greenwich Park, home to the National Maritime Museum, the Old Royal Observatory and the site of the 0° meridian line (both old and newly calculated versions). A working city farm and the former inland docks to the north are accessed via an old dockers foot tunnel that runs beneath the River Thames.

1 **Blackheath** During the deadly plagues of 1348 and 1665 that swept across London, many large burial pits were created close to populated areas. It is an urban myth that a huge burial site was created here and the name Blackheath originated from this, however, the name is much older and refers either to the darkness of the soil or the bleak aspect of the heathland. Blackheath is 86ha of raised, open green space with very few trees to interrupt the views. An ancient route, now the A2, from London to Canterbury, cuts across the heath.

The dryness of the land and its ease of access to the Thames has made it popular with early settlers. Evidence of Stone Age tools have been unearthed on the heath along with Roman and Viking settlements.

Blackheath was once an ancient wild heathland covered with heather and gorse and it was reckoned to have contained more species of grass than anywhere else in the south of England. Today, it has more uniform grasses for the sports pitches. Over the past two centuries, as London has expanded, much of the wildlife has been chased away, though chiffchaffs can still be seen along with stag beetles and lesser marsh grasshoppers.

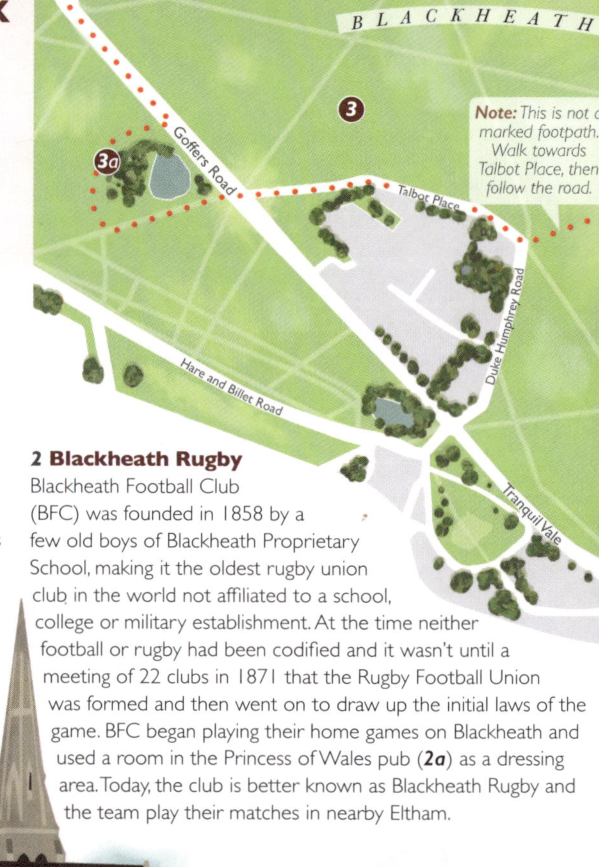

2 Blackheath Rugby

Blackheath Football Club (BFC) was founded in 1858 by a few old boys of Blackheath Proprietary School, making it the oldest rugby union club in the world not affiliated to a school, college or military establishment. At the time neither football or rugby had been codified and it wasn't until a meeting of 22 clubs in 1871 that the Rugby Football Union was formed and then went on to draw up the initial laws of the game. BFC began playing their home games on Blackheath and used a room in the Princess of Wales pub (**2a**) as a dressing area. Today, the club is better known as Blackheath Rugby and the team play their matches in nearby Eltham.

3 A place of gathering and revolt

For thousands of years, armies and large crowds gathered on the heath. Its dry terrain, good visibility and access to the river made it a strategic place to encamp. The Roman army certainly stopped here, possibly in AD 43, before heading further west to cross the Thames.

The Middle Ages saw several uprisings of working people against the monarch and the government. In 1381, when the young Richard II imposed an extra three groat tax, working men of 28 counties, led by Wat Tyler, rose up against this duty and 10,000 men assembled on Blackheath ready to march on the capital.

Discontent grew over the government of Henry VI and issues of corruption, abuse of power and higher taxes to fight the Hundred Year War, leading to a popular revolt in the south-east of England. In 1450, a gathering of 20,000 people of Kent and Essex, led by Jack Cade, encamped on Blackheath before heading west with a view to overthrowing the establishment. In both revolts, Tyler and Cade were executed by the establishment and their followers dispersed.

The followers of Thomas Flannock and Michael Joseph were not so lucky. In 1497, the two leaders led a large group of Cornishmen, unhappy with higher taxes imposed to pay for a war with the Scots, who camped on Blackheath, ready to march on London. Henry VII sent his army to disperse or kill the rebels. In the ensuing Battle of Blackheath about 2,000 insurgents were killed. It is alleged that many of the bodies were dumped in what is now Whitefield Mount (*3a*) just behind Whitefield Pond.

Left: medieval rebels gather on Blackheath. Far left: All Saints' Church and a group of school children playing rugby on the wide open space of Blackheath.

1 Queen Caroline's bath The marriage of Princess Caroline of Brunswick to her cousin, the Prince Regent (later George IV), in 1795, was not a happy one. The prince was far more interested in his mistress and he spread rumours of Caroline's unchaste behaviour and lack of hygiene. Within a year they were living separate lives with the princess removed to Montague House in Greenwich. When she left the country in 1814, George had the house torn down. This bath was discovered in 1909 and later excavated in 2001. Perhaps Caroline wasn't as unhygienic as her husband reported.

2 The London Marathon start line Each year the 26.2-mile-long race, which attacts 49,000 runners, commences on Blackheath. To avoid congestion, there are three starting points: Charlton Way, Shooter's Hill Road and St John's Park. The first London Marathon was held in 1981.

3 Greenwich Park In 1437, Henry VI gave his uncle, Humphrey, Duke of Gloucester, a section of the northern heath that ran down to the Thames. Humphrey then set about landscaping this 74ha piece of now royal parkland and creating a new royal abode, Bella Court, later named the

Palace of Placentia (or Pleasant Place). It was constructed close to the river, where the Old Royal Naval College now stands. Humphrey created a huge library of books, which on his death was transferred to Oxford and became the nucleus of the Bodleian Library.

Many English monarchs preferred to site their palaces close to the River Thames (Hampton Court, Whitehall and Windsor Castle), as it was faster and offered greater security when travelling. Several monarchs were born at the Palace of Placentia, including Henry VIII, Elizabeth I and Mary Tudor. Henry VIII introduced deer to the park in 1515, to enable him to pursue one of his favourite pastimes, deer hunting. Greenwich Park was originally ringed with a high wooden fence to keep the deer in and the commoners out. James I replaced the wooden fence with a brick wall, some of which still stands today.

During the English Civil War, Charles II fled to France. While there, he will have encountered the work of French landscape designer André Le Nôtre. Upon Charles' restoration to the English throne in 1660, he commissioned Le Nôtre to create plans for Greenwich Park. Le Nôtre was at this time designing the Gardens of Versailles for Louis XIV. Several avenues of chestnut trees planted at this time are still in place today. The park now contains over 4,000 trees, including sweet chestnuts, cedars, hawthorns and common oaks. Sadly, a number of trees have succumbed to infections, ageing and squirrel damage, although many are being replaced.

Clockwise from left: a horse chestnut tree lined avenue within Greenwich Park; Queen Caroline's bath within the former Montague House; runners at the start line of the London Marathon.

Walking these pages 1.7km

1 **Queen Elizabeth's Oak** It is believed that this fallen oak was planted in the 12th century and died in 1900. It remained upright until 1991 when a gale toppled it. A replacement oak has been planted close by.

2 The View The panoramic view *(see above)* from the statue of General Wolfe is probably the finest view in London and requires some time to take it all in. Starting in the north-west is the City of London and St Paul's Cathedral. Down across the grassy slope is the Queen's House and just beyond are the twin baroque palaces that became the former Royal Naval Hospital. Looming across the River Thames are the ever-rising tower blocks of Canary Wharf, while to the north-east you'll see the O2 Arena and the four chimneys of Greenwich Power Station (a back-up generator for the London Underground network).

3 The meridian line The structure to the east of Flamsteed House is today named The Meridian Building and was constructed in 1720. As the 19th century progressed, the need for greater accuracy in timekeeping increased. Shipping required precise timepieces to aide navigation and, later, the railways would need to run on a standard time across the country. In 1884, an international conference in Washington, DC voted to set the Prime Meridian (0 degrees longitude) in Greenwich. The original meridian line had been calculated by George Airy in 1851, as running north-south from his office adjacent to Flamsteed

Above: the view of London from the northern end of Blackheath Avenue. Below left: Flamsteed House with the red 'navigation' sphere.

House, and so he set the Greenwich meridian line here. A new line is now set within the grounds of the Meridian House, where, for the price of admission, you can stand with one foot in the eastern hemisphere and one in the west. However, improved GPS technology has revealed that the true line is actually 102.5m to the east (**3a**), though this is not marked within the park.

4 The Old Royal Observatory

Charles II was a major benefactor of the sciences during his reign. In 1675, he appointed John Flamsteed as Astronomer Royal. A section of l and was provided in Greenwich Park to build the new observatory and Sir Christopher Wren and Robert Hooke were appointed to design what would become known as Flamsteed House. Funding for the Royal Observatory was in short supply, so materials had to be salvaged from a Tower of London gatehouse, meaning some of the 'stonework' is actually timber. Flamsteed had to purchase his own telescope despite royal enthusiasm for the project. His successor was Edmund Halley. Halley went on to calculate in 1705 that a comet, which had been sighted by many over the years, was in fact rotating around the solar system and it would reappear every 76 years. The comet is named after him.

In 1833, a red ball on a shaft was added to the roof of Flamsteed House. At 1pm each day the ball would drop to indicate the times, enabling mariners on the Thames to accurately set their chronometers. This was vital for precise navigation. The ball still drops every day at the given time. Following the Second World War, the Royal Observatory moved away from the increasing bright lights and pollution of London to Herstmonceux in East Sussex. Today, Flamsteed House is a museum.

5 National Maritime Museum

This building was created in 1807, as an extension to the Royal Naval Hospital. Since 1934 it has become home to the National Maritime Museum, sited appropriately in Greenwich and close to the River Thames. The galleries are festooned with paintings and models of old ships; military, mercantile and exploratory. There are also many uniforms on display, including the one worn by Nelson when he was fatally shot at the Battle of Trafalgar. The museum is free to enter.

6 Queen's House

In 1616, James I commissioned the architect Inigo Jones to create a two-storey Palladian-style house for his wife, Anne of Denmark, to keep her art collection. Sadly, she never lived to see it completed and the King called a halt to the work. The project was resumed following instruction by Charles I and was completed in 1637, who donated it to his wife, Henrietta Maria. The main hall was designed as a perfect cube. The house was the first Palladian structure to be built in England and was considered radical at the time. In 1649, Charles I was deposed by Cromwell's government and later beheaded. Following the Restoration, Charles II had the building restored and redeveloped. Over the past two centuries it was used as a Royal Hospital School for the sons of seamen and today it houses the art collection of the National Maritime Museum.

1 The Old Royal Naval Hospital

Following the English Civil War, Charles II instigated the restoration of the damaged Queen's House and created a whole new waterfront palace. A former palace on this site had seen the births of Henry VIII and Elizabeth I.

John Webb, son-in-law of Inigo Jones, was commissioned to create a Baroque palace. However, following the death of Charles II in 1685, William III took the throne. His preference was to live much further upstream at Hampton Court. His wife, Mary II, dedicated the new palace to the care of retired and disabled seamen. She had been moved by the sight of injured sailors following the 1692 Battle of La Hogue and wanted to create a naval counterpart to the army hospital in Chelsea that had been established by Charles II.

Sir Christopher Wren continued the work started by Webb and created another palace to the east which was a mirror image of the initial palace, with the Queen's House being framed between the two when viewed from the river. For those heading to London by water the grand sight of domes, columns and palaces would be the first buildings that they encountered – a symbol of England's state and naval power. The first naval pensioners began moving here in 1704 while work was still in progress.

When Wren died in 1723, his two assistants, Nicholas Hawksmoor and Sir John Vanbrugh, took over the project. The hospital finally closed in 1869 and was converted into a naval college. In 1998 the building became part of the University of Greenwich.

2 St Alfege Church

In 1012, Alfege, the then Archbishop of Canterbury, was kidnapped by Vikings in Kent and taken to Greenwich, where they demanded a huge cash ransom. The Archbishop refused to pay and eventually his pagan captors beat him to death on what would become the site of this church. Alfege was later canonised in 1078.

Thomas Tallis, one of England's finest composers, was the organist between 1540 and

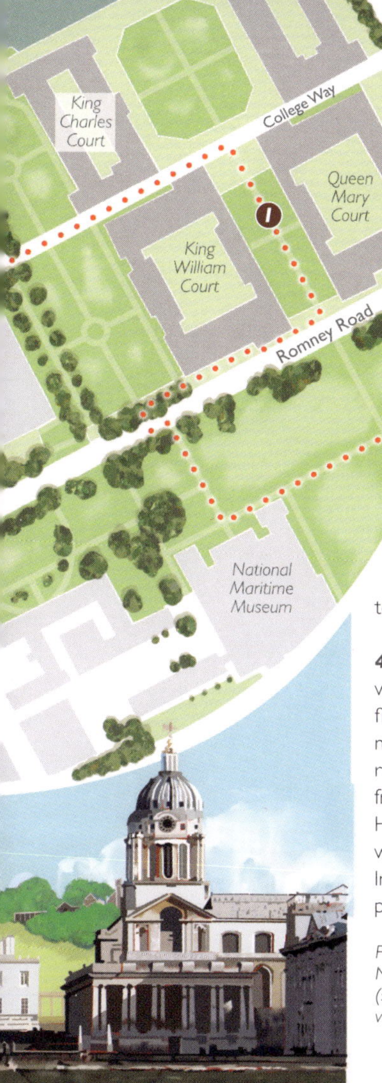

1585 in the earlier church on this site and was buried here. The current church was designed by Nicholas Hawksmoor in 1712, in a very grand Baroque style.

3 Greenwich Village

Long before English royalty, their palaces and the meridian line arrived, this location, on a bend in the Thames, was named Grenewic by the Anglo-Saxons. And for many hundreds of years the main economic activity here was fishing. Up until the late 19th century, Greenwich was renowned for serving whitebait dinners in its pubs and restaurants. Today, with the aforementioned royal palaces, park, numerous historic naval features and its UNESCO World Heritage Site rating, Greenwich has become a major London tourist attraction.

4 Cutty Sark

Cutty Sark, a clipper sailing ship, was commissioned in 1869 and embarked on its first voyage from Shanghai to London, carrying mainly tea. Though *Cutty Sark* never won the 'tea race', it did break the record for carrying wool from Australia, once covering 672km in 24 hours. However, this was to be the last 'hurrah' of the wind-powered boats in the commercial world. In 1869, the Suez Canal opened and steam-powered shipping shortened sea journey times, which were no longer reliant on variable winds.

Cutty Sark continued working as the last clipper operating in the world until 1922. The vessel later became a training ship before its retirement when it was restored and finally displayed at Greenwich in 1957. During a further restoration in 2007, *Cutty Sark* was damaged by fire. The ship is now repaired and on permanent display by the Thames.

From left to right: St Alfege's Church; the Old Royal Naval Hospital as viewed from Island Gardens (see next page); Cutty Sark encased within a visitor centre.

1 The Greenwich Foot Tunnel By the end of the 19th century dockers heading from Greenwich to work on the Isle of Dogs found crossing the Thames by ferry unreliable and crowded. So, a foot tunnel, designed by Sir Alexander Binnie (he'd also designed the Vauxhall Bridge and the first Blackwall Tunnel), was built under the Thames. The cast iron tunnel is lined with 200,000 tiles and is 370m long. It can be accessed by both lift and a spiral staircase and is open 24 hours a day. In the tunnel during quieter periods, one can hear sound of boat propellers going overhead.

2 Island Gardens At the exit of the foot tunnel is a small riverside garden with one of the great views in London. Across the river, on the opposite shore, are the old Naval College buildings, with The Queen's House and Greenwich Park in the distance, all symmetrically aligned (see *previous page*). The view that the Italian artist Giovanni Caneletto painted around 1750 has hardly changed over the centuries.

3 Millwall Park The Isle of Dogs was once an area of treeless marshland, which the Thames would frequently flood. During the 17th century, walls were constructed around the 'island' shoreline and are still in place today. Windmills were also constructed to pump the water out and keep the Isle of Dogs dry.

4 Millwall FC The Millwall Rovers football club, as it was originally known, was founded in 1885 on the Isle of Dogs by workers of C&E Morton's canning factory. The team played on several pitches in Millwall, including here in Millwall Park, until 1910, when they moved across the Thames to a larger ground, The Den, in Bermondsey, although the club retained the name Millwall. Later, in 1993, the club relocated to The New Den, where the team still plays today.

5 Mudchute Park and Farm

When Millwall Dock was being created in the 1860s, the earth from the excavations was removed by liquefying the spoil, pumping it pneumatically through a conduit (or mudchute) and depositing it in this area of Cubitt Town. The pipe would later give its name to the park. The 13ha park, established in 1977, is now the largest urban farm in Europe. It is home to around 100 farm animals and has a remote and rural feel to the place, that is until you notice the gleaming towers of Canary Wharf just to the north. The farm is free to visit but voluntary donations are very welcome.

6 Millwall Dock

Millwall Dock opened in 1868, a relative latecomer to the London Docklands (the huge West India Docks, just north of this point, had opened some 60 years earlier). The 14ha Millwall Dock specialised in the import of fresh produce, grain, timber and alcohol. However, initial plans for the dock had to be severely curtailed as competition from new docks in the north of England was becoming noticable. In 1909, Millwall Dock merged with several other docks under the newly formed Port of London Authority. By the 1970s, all the London docks had become redundant, as large container ships could no longer navigate the shallow waters of the Thames. Today, the inverted L-shaped inland dock is used as a sailing and watersports facility and is surrounded by mainly residential apartments.

Clockwise from far left: a map of the Isle of Dogs circa 1960; the Greenwich Foot Tunnel; the north entrance to the tunnel; Mudchute Park and Farm with Canary Wharf behind.

Walking these pages 2.6km

Opposite: view of central London and the City from One Tree Hill.

PECKHAM – CRYSTAL PALACE

The three-hill walk begins on Peckham Rye and rises quickly onto One Tree Hill, then onwards to Sydenham Hill and the site of the former Crystal Palace. The effort is worth it as you'll be rewarded incredible views over the capital and the south-east.

PECKHAM – CRYSTAL PALACE

Total walking distance 13.1km

This undulating walk commences on the flatlands of Peckham and rises quickly onto One Tree Hill. The ascent is worth the effort for the views offered of the City and St Paul's Cathedral. There are several other great vistas to be seen along this route, too, which will take you over several hills in south London, through ancient woods, along former railway lines, past a magnificent museum and out onto the vast sloping park of Crystal Palace.

1 Peckham The south London settlement of Peckham is referred to in the Domesday Book of 1086 as Pecheha (*peak-ham*), meaning 'a village among the hills'. It remained a rural community until the 19th century, when, in 1865, the railway arrived. The open fields and market gardens soon disappeared beneath new housing for working people who could now commute to work in central London. In the 1960s, several modern high-rise flats were built in North Peckham. Following an economic downturn in the 1970s, as employment opportunities disappeared the estate became one of the most deprived in the country. Investment from the European Union in the 1990s helped improve the housing stock and social amenities, and today it is one of the most ethnically diverse districts in the UK. Like many of the districts of London, gentrification is having its effect on Peckham, with new alternative shops, restaurants and businesses springing up.

2 Peckham Rye Common and Park The 44ha park and the common together form an isosceles triangle with the common to the north and the park to the south, and comprises of grassland, meadow, ornamental gardens, lakes, woodlands and a river.

The common was traditionally a space for drovers to rest their cattle in holding pens, while en route to market from the Kentish farms. The Kentish Drovers pub, on Peckham High Street takes its name from an old inn that stood on the opposite side of the road and was once a watering hole for the cattle drovers.

In the late 1860s, after much concern about the common being misappropriated for private use, the Camberwell Vestry purchased it and, in 1882, transferred ownership to the Metropolitan Board of Works. Peckham Rye Park opened in 1894, created out of farmland to provide open green space for south Londoners.

The ornamental

grounds in the park were designed in the style of an 'Old English garden'. This was later named the Sexby Garden (*2a*) after John J Sexby, London County Council's first Chief Officer of Parks and designer of this park. During Sexby's time as COP he was responsible for the creation and development of many London parks, including Ruskin Park, Golders Hill Park (page 30) and Springfield Park (page 64). A Japanese garden (*2b*) was opened close to the Sexby Garden in 1908. The park's woodland comprises of London plane, horse chestnut, oak, ash and crack willow and some non-native trees such as Persian ironwood.

Peckham Rye Park was used during the Second World War to house Italian prisoners of war. Here they grew vegetables and reared chickens and pigs on the common. One of the POW huts was used for a pre-school club until around 2018, when it was demolished.

William Blake's vision In 1767, ten-year-old William Blake would walk from the family home in Soho to Peckham Rye Common (a round trip of 19km). It was on one of his journeys here that he claimed to have seen a vision of 'a tree filled with angels, bright angelic wings bespangling every bough like stars'. The artist and poet continued to see such visions throughout his life.

3 River Peck The River Peck rises in several springs on One Tree Hill and then flows northwards through a conduit, until it reaches Peckham Rye Park where, exposed, it meanders through the landscaped park for about half a kilometre until reaching the common. Here it ventures back underground again, joins up with the Earl's Sluice in South Bermondsey and enters the Thames in Rotherhithe. In the days when it was a fully opened, shallow stream, it offered very little transportation use and nor was it powerful enough to drive mill wheels. Consequently, it never attracted heavy industry and, unlike many of London's counterparts, it never became totally polluted and the short stretch through Peckham Rye Park was left exposed. However, the need for land was so great that the rest of the Peck was covered over in 1820s. On the common there are two manhole covers where the river can sometimes be heard flowing beneath.

Far left: a solitary London plane tree on Peckham Rye Common.
Above: the Wisteria pergola, within Sexby Garden.

1 Honor Oak Reservoir Beneath a nine-hole golf course is a massive water reservoir with a capacity of 270,000 cubic metres. When it was built by the Southwark and Vauxhall Water Company in 1909, it was the largest brick-built water store in the world. The clay excavated to create this storage unit was used to create the bricks from which it was built. The River Peck runs by the reservoir but does not feed into it. The reservoir was originally fed by a well, though it is now part of the Thames Water Ring Main.

Croydon to Southwark and its trees were vital in suppling timber to the Royal Dockyards on the Thames.

In the 1580s, a fire beacon was located here. It was one of a chain of such signals used to notify the military of a potential Spanish invasion (the Spanish Armada would arrive in the English Channel in 1588). The East India Company placed a semaphore signal station here to transmit news of shipping on the south coast.

For centuries this area was deemed to be common land. In 1896, a fence was suddenly erected around the perimeter to keep people out. A long campaign by The Enclosure of Honor Oak Hill Protest Committee was fought to keep One Tree Hill in public ownership. Finally, in 1905, after protests and legal challenges the hill was taken into public ownership.

A concrete platform (**3a**), which is still in place, was the base for anti-Zeppelin guns used during the First World War. The vista through the break in the trees to the north offers a commanding view of the London skyline, including the City of London, St Paul's Cathedral and the Shard.

4 Oak of Honor It is believed that Elizabeth I was invited by a courtier to picnic here at this location on 1 May 1602, and that the tree, the Oak of Honor, was named after the event. However, the royal springtime lunch may have occurred down the hill in Peckham. The current Oak of

2 Railway embankment On the corner of Brenchley Gardens and Kelvington Road there is a grassy embankment that, until the 1950s, carried the Crystal Palace to Nunhead railway line. Following the Crystal Palace fire in 1936, the railway's popularity declined and it was eventually closed.

3 One Tree Hill The name is very misleading as the area is heavily wooded, having once been part of the ancient Great North Wood that covered a large section of south London. It stretched from

Honor was planted in the early 1900s and is protected by metal railings. Other trees on the hill include London planes, hawthorns and black poplars.

5 St Augustine's Church

This Grade II-listed church is built of Kentish ragstone and was consecrated in 1872. The tower was added in 1886. St Augustine's appears quite secluded during the summer when the trees are in full leaf and it is impossible to view from the road below.

6 Camberwell Old Cemetery

As the population of London began to grow exponentially during the 19th century, the need for more graveyards beyond central London became more acute. The first wave of new cemetery construction saw the likes of Highgate and Abney Park (page 59) being established. However, by the 1840s, it was becoming apparent that these 'Magnificent Seven' cemeteries were not sufficient and that more burial grounds were needed. Encouraged by government legislation, the Camberwell Cemetery Board purchased this 12ha site in 1855, with the first interment occurring a year later. Frederick J Horniman, of the Horniman Museum, was buried here in 1906. And there is also a memorial, erected in 1920, to members of the public who were killed during a Zeppelin raid.

By the late 20th century and after 300,000 burials, the cemetery was full. Three gothic chapels, designed by the architectural firm of Gilbert Scott, were constructed here for burial services. Once this graveyard neared capacity, the chapels were neglected, fell into decline and were later demolished. The nearby Camberwell New Cemetery was opened in 1927 to eventually replace the 'old' cemetery once it was full.

Clockwise from the far left: the view of London and the City over the One Tree Hill canopy; the Oak of Honor; the access point into the Honor Oak Reservoir.

Walking these pages 2.6km

1 Horniman Nature Trail

The trail is situated on the former Crystal Palace and South London Junction Railway line, which opened in 1865 to ferry visitors to and from Crystal Palace. The line closed in 1954 and, in 1972, was transformed into this nature trail, the first of its type in London. The trail should connect Camberwell Old Cemetery to the Horniman Museum and Gardens. However, the gates on Langton Rise are permanently closed, making the northern end of the trail a cul-de-sac.

2 Horniman Gardens

On a clear day from the bandstand within these gardens there is a fabulous view of the capital's skyline. The park includes a variety of gardens: rock, sunken and African. The Ecological Centre has a grassed-over roof.

3 Horniman Museum

Frederick J Horniman (1835–1906) was the head of the Horniman Tea company, a social reformer and, from 1895, the Liberal Party MP for Penryn and Falmouth. During his global travels Horniman amassed a large collection of art and natural history artefacts. Beginning in late 1890, he opened his house in Forest Hill for several days a week to display some of his 350,000 objects to the public. Surrey House museum, as it became known, welcomed half a million visitors in the first eight years. In 1898, Horniman had the house demolished to make way for a permanent museum.

The new structure was designed by Charles Harrison Townsend in an Art Nouveau style with sandstone and red brick (Harrison also designed the Whitechapel Art Gallery in the East End of London). It featured what quickly became an iconic curved clock tower. The Horniman Museum opened in 1901 and along with its

6ha of parkland it was presented to the London County Council as a gift to the people of the capital.

Humanity on the House of Circumstance, a neoclassical mosaic by Robert Anning Bell adjacent to the clock tower, depicts the course of human life and consists of 117,000 tile pieces. It was assembled by a group of young women over a 210-day period. The museum has continued to expand and grow throughout the 20th century. The Grade II-listed museum and gardens are free to enter.

4 Sydenham Hill Wood In the 1980s the wood was threatened due to plans to build houses upon it. The trees and land, saved from the bulldozer, are now managed by the London Wildlife Trust. The managed path through Sydenham Hill Wood is a continuation of the Horniman Trail and follows the former Crystal Palace railway line. The area, along with Dulwich Wood, is a large fragment of the former Great North Wood and is populated with willow, elm, sessile oak and hornbeam.

More exotic trees, such as cedar of Lebanon, have grown here in the past 150 years. These once stood in the grounds of the grand houses that lined Sydenham Hill. Having been demolished, the gardens were absorbed into the wood.

On the footbridge (**4a**) over the former railway line was where, in 1871, Camille Pissarro painted the view of Lordship Lane Station, Dulwich. The station has long gone and the view has changed dramatically, arguably for the better. The painting is now on display in the Courtauld Gallery, London. The wooden footbridge, following recent repairs, is once again accessible to the public.

The entrance to Crescent Wood railway tunnel (**4b**), at the southern end of Sydenham Hill Wood, is now used as a bat roost that includes several pipistrelle species. The tunnel was built with bricks fired on site using local London clay.

Clockwise from above: Lordship Lane Station, Dulwich, painted by Camille Pissarro; the bandstand in Horniman Gardens; a taxidermied walrus displayed in the Horniman Museum; the Horniman Museum clock tower; an architectural folly found in Sydenham Hill Wood.

1 John Logie Baird In 1926, the prolific inventor John Logie Baird publicly demonstrated the first working television in London. Eight years later he had established a television laboratory within Crystal Palace and was broadcasting limited test programmes independent of the BBC. Baird was living nearby at 3 Crescent Wood Road and his company aimed to start regular television transmissions from Crystal Palace. However, the 1936 fire (see opposite) proved a huge setback, and by this time the BBC had acquired television studios across London in Alexandra Palace (page 47). There is a plaque commemorating Baird on the house in Crescent Wood Road.

2 Sydenham Wells Park The efficacious qualities of a well within this park reached the ear of George III, who made several visits during his reign (1760–1820) to drink the waters. One of the wells is now covered by Well Park Road but several others are still active and feed the pond. By the beginning of the 20th century the park had been acquired by the Metropolitan Board of Works and landscaped with ornamental beds, a lake and footpaths. It was opened in 1901 by John Burns, MP for Battersea and one of the first Independent Labour Party members in the House of Commons.

3 The Maze With a diameter of nearly 50m, this is one of the largest mazes in the country. It first opened in the 1870s and is still in use today.

4 Crystal Palace Bowl The Bowl, which opened in 1961, has hosted many musical acts as diverse as Pink Floyd, Vera Lynn, The Beach Boys and Nigel Kennedy. Bob Marley and the Wailers played here in June 1980. It was their largest UK concert and would be Marley's last performance in the UK. A Nubian Jak Community Trust plaque commemorates this event. Marley died less than a year later of a melanoma, at the age of 36.

5 Arqiva Transmitting Station

This very tall mast (219m), visible from many parts of London, serves a vital function of transmitting TV and radio signals to most of the capital. It first began operating in 1956, when it took over from the aerial at Alexandra Palace (page 47). It was used to test early colour television broadcasts. The transmitter here was built on the site of John Logie Baird's test television studio and mast.

6 Crystal Palace Following the Great Exhibition in 1851 (page 19), the massive iron and glass edifice was dismantled and rebuilt on an area then known as Penge Peak. In 1854, the Crystal Palace reopened and the 80ha grounds that it stood in became known as Crystal Palace Park and for over 80 years, the 4,000-capacity exhibition centre, continued to entertain with exhibitions and concerts. It was, at over 560m long and 124m wide, the largest indoor space in the world. Two ornate water towers flanked each end of the palace to power the fountains.

However, on the night of 30 November 1936, a small fire quickly spread. The dry wooden floors burned quickly and the glass panes exploded in the heat. Many thousands gathered to witness the fire and it was claimed that its glow could be seen over 60km away. The fire brigade were overwhelmed and unable to save the building, and all that remained were the foundations, two water towers, three pairs of concrete sphinxes and the lower Italian terraces (**6a**). The water towers were later removed. The space occupied by the Palace is still empty, despite several proposals to reuse the site. The tall Arqiva transmitter was constructed in 1956, very close to the site.

Clockwise from left: the iron and glass Crystal Palace before its destruction by fire in November 1936; the Crystal Palace maze; one of the concrete Sphinxes, now painted dark pink, which survived the fire.

1 The View Most of the great panoramic views featured in this guidebook are of central London and the City. This south-east outlook from the Crystal Palace Italianate terraces, however, gives views towards Bromley, Orpington and the Weald of Kent beyond.

2 The Lower & Upper Italian Terraces These two Italian terraces are, along with the three pairs of sphinxes, are all that survived the great fire of 1936. Opened in 1854, the terraces once overlooked ornate gardens laid out by the designer of the Great Exhibition, Sir Joseph Paxton. These Grade II-listed balconies are now deteriorating and in need of restoration.

3 The Paxton statue When the large bust of Sir Joseph Paxton (1803–1865) was first revealed in 1873, on the 20th anniversary of the Palace's opening, it was facing towards the massive structure. Following the destructive fire, the bust was re-sited on a brick plinth and now faces away from the site of the former Crystal Palace structure (perhaps he can't bear to look). The bust was created in Carrera marble by the sculptor WF Woodington in 1869.

4 National Sport Centre The National Sports Centre was built over the site where the FA Cup final was held each year from 1895 to 1914. In the last final played here Burnley beat Liverpool 1-0. The finals moved to the Empire Stadium (now known as Wembley Stadium) in 1923. Crystal Palace FC was founded here in 1905, but the army commandeered the park during the First World War. By 1924, the club was eventually established a few

5 Crystal Palace Dinosaurs The dinosaur park was created in 1852, in an age when the study of palaeontology was still in its infancy. Consequently, some of the creatures on display are crude representations of what we know about dinosaurs today. Only four of the 29 creatures displayed are true dinosaurs, the rest are early mammals such as crocodilians and pterosaurs.

6 Crystal Palace Park Farm This is a small working farm and college within the park and is very popular with children and parents (admission is free but donations are welcome). The farm features pigs and sheep, goats and rabbits, plus more exotic creatures such as meerkats, snakes and lizards. It is open every afternoon except Wednesdays.

Clockwise from left: a section of the Italian Terrace with the disfigured statue of Dante and the Arqiva transmitter beyond; an iguanodon, one of the Crystal Palace dinosaurs; a bust of Sir Joseph Paxton.

kilometres to the south, at its current home, Selhurst Park. The National Sports Centre opened in 1964 with a seating capacity of 16,000, which can be increased by 4,000 with temporary seating. It is best known as an athletics arena for both national and international events. There is also an indoor sports complex that includes a 50m pool plus a sport arena for gymnastics and basketball.

The outdoor sport facility is also used as a contemporary music venue. The likes of Bruce Springsteen and the Sex Pistols have performed here over the past 50 years.

Wetland
Boardwalk
MORDEN HALL
PARK
South Wimbledon
Merton
Mitcham
LAMBETH
CEMETERY

THE LOWER WANDLE VALLEY

On this river walk once stood an Augustinian church the size of Westminster Cathedral and an influential Arts and Crafts workshop. Although neither is still standing, some remains are visible.

Right: The Wetland Boardwalk

THE LOWER WANDLE VALLEY

Total walking distance 9.5km

The fast-flowing Wandle rises in Croydon and heads northwards to the Thames. Over the past 400 years it has transformed from being a clean chalk stream to a heavily industrialised and polluted waterway. Today, it is recovering, though it is not quite back to bucolic levels.

River Wandle The River Wandle, a chalk stream, is one of London's few uncovered rivers. It rises on the North Downs, near Croydon, and heads almost due north to reach the Thames at Wandsworth. It drops 28m over its 19km course, so is a fairly fast-flowing stream, which proved to be very useful for powering watermills. The Domesday Book of 1086 listed 13 mills on the river. By the end of the 19th century, the river was driving over 90 mills, which were producing many goods including paper, textiles, gunpowder, corn, copper, linseed oil and snuff. Prior to the advent of the steam engine, the river had more water mills per kilometre than probably anywhere else in the UK and therefore was one of the most industrialised waterways. Its usefulness likely prevented it being covered over; a humiliation that befell many central London rivers.

As steam and later electricity superseded waterpower, the nature of the industries changed to those of paint and chemicals production, with many factories using the river as a disposal facility. Consequently, by the 1960s the waterway was declared a sewer.

Since the 1990s, many of the polluting industries have either ceased trading or moved away, and parliamentary legislation regarding water quality has improved matters. The establishment of groups such as the Wandle Trust, the Wandsworth Society and the Wandle Valley Regional Park, along with volunteers and local councils, have commenced the work of creating new green spaces and cleaning up the river. In 2011, the Environment Agency named the Wandle one of the most improved rivers in England and Wales, and the river is now much cleaner and supports the likes of freshwater shrimps, brown trout, eels and herons.

1 Morden Hall Park Morden Hall (*1a*) was built around 1770 for the Garth family as a residence, after which it was converted into a private school for 'young gentlemen'. This establishment closed in 1840. In 1872, the owner, Sir Richard Garth, sold the house and the 50ha estate, including a deer park, to Gilliat Hatfeild, owner of the adjacent

the Victorian era, was commonly believed to have therapeutic qualities. It became especially popular during the Great Plague of 1665 and later among the elite; George IV, Admiral Lord Nelson, the Duke of Wellington and Benjamin Disraeli were all noted partakers. Meanwhile, the working classes made do with smoking tobacco. Today, a ceremonial communal snuff box is still in place by the entrance to House of Commons, though rarely used.

The fast-flowing Wandle enabled the mill wheels to grind the dried tobacco leaves into snuff and, unlike textile production, the work required relatively few staff. The river was re-engineered in places to create mill ponds and a stream to maximise the power of the water. Locally grown lavender and peppermint were added to flavour the snuff. It was Hatfeild's son, also named Gilliat, who continued the snuff grinding business into the 20th century. Even though he was seen as a fair and just employer, when his staff joined a national cigarette industry strike, he closed the factory down not long afterwards, in 1922.

snuff mill. During the First World War, Morden Hall was used as a military hospital.

On his death in 1941, Gilliat Hatfeild junior bequeathed the hall and estate to the National Trust, which continues to manage the estate and parkland through which the Wandle meanders. Morden Hall is today privately leased and not open to the public. However, Hatfeild did stipulate that access to the grounds be free.

2 The Snuff Mill

There has been a snuff mill on this site since around 1750. The Taddy family took over the lease in 1845. Within a decade, Alexander Hatfeild had married into the family, and by 1854 he was running the successful business.

The snorting of tobacco-based snuff, fashionable from the 17th century until the end of

Far left: the remaining Snuff Mill wheel. Left: Morden Hall.

1 The Wetland Boardwalk

This is the remains of a river floodplain and the ingress of water has encouraged a rich biodiversity. A series of recently opened boardwalks zigzag over an area of wetlands that is fed by the Wandle. The viewing platforms, by the ponds, are a great place to spot newts, frogs, moorhens, reed warblers and herons within the reed beds.

2 Deen City Farm

Located on the site of a calico bleaching area, Deen City Farm is a 2ha working farm, riding school and educational resource that teaches urban dwelling children about the rural world. The farm is home to numerous domesticated animals including ducks, goats, geese, chickens and horses. It opened in 1994 and admission is free.

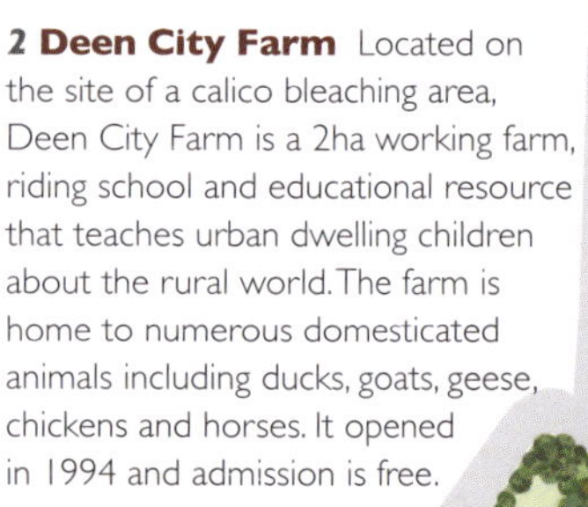

3 Merton Abbey Mills

There is a reference to two mills operating in this area in the Domesday Book of 1086. In 1870, Edmund Littler established a textile printing works here. Five years later, Arthur Liberty opened his shop, Liberty & Co, on Regent Street. It specialised in selling fabrics and furnishings from the Far East. However, supply and reliability became an issue, so Liberty looked closer to home for printed silk textiles and found it on the banks of the Wandle at the Littler printshop.

Nearly all of Littler's hand-printed output of paisley and Art Nouveau fabrics would be sold by Liberty's. Eventually, in 1904, Liberty's bought the company and built a new 'Long Shop'. This housed the extended printing tables and supplied good natural light for colour matching and alignment. But on a darker note, the company was responsible for a huge amount of chemicals, including sulphuric acid, alum and chloride of lime, which were used to clean the fabrics. These chemicals were then flushed into the river, giving the fish no chance of survival. The river was effectively dead.

Textile printing continued here until the early 1980s, when the factory closed. In 1989, Merton Abbey Mills were converted into a visitor centre and a theatre, and the Long Shop is home to a craft market and restaurant.

Merton Place

About 400m to the north-west of Merton Abbey Mills once stood the house Merton Place. This was, for two years from 1801, Admiral Lord Nelson's London home, where he lived with his mistress Emma Hamilton and

her husband. The house stood within a 40ha estate, complete with its own waterway; a stream taken off the Wandle and nicknamed the Nile. It was here that Nelson learned to catch trout with his one remaining arm (his right arm had been amputated after he was shot during the Battle of Santa Cruz de Tenerife in 1797). In 1803, hostilities resumed with France and Nelson returned to sea. He was killed two years later at the Battle of Trafalgar.

4 The Wheelhouse The Wheelhouse, with its seven-spoke mill wheel known as an undershot wheel, was constructed in the 1860s for the process of rinsing silk after it had been printed. More recently, the mill wheel once powered pottery wheels and today it generates a small amount of electricity. It is the only working mill wheel on the Wandle and features on the London Borough of Merton's logo (page 124).

5 The Archway This replica structure constructed in 1988, close to a Norman arch that was once part of the garden entrance to Abbey House located south of the Merantun Way. Medieval walls can still be seen close to this arch.

Eels The Wandle has seen the reintroduction of eels over recent years and is now one of the better rivers in the UK to support eels. The river has had its weirs specially adapted with tiles that enable the eels to navigate up the river from the Thames and grow to maturity before eventually returning to the Sargasso Sea, 5,000km away, where they then breed and die. Freshwater fish such as chub, roach, dace and gudgeon have been introduced to the Wandle as water quality has improved over the past few decades. However, the river still suffers from occasional 'accidental' pollution incidents.

Clockwise from top right: a replica Norman gateway; the Long Shop, a former Morris print works in Merton Abbey Mills; the Wetland Boardwalk; a pair of eels.

1 Merton Priory A religious community of Augustinian monks was established at this location in 1117, by Gilbert, Sheriff of Surrey with land granted to him by Henry I. This became a vital ecclesiastical site with a large priory. The priory church was the size of Westminster Cathedral (100m in length). In 1236, Henry III met with various earls, bishops and the Archbishop of Canterbury to discuss 'the common good of the realm'. The resulting Statute of Merton was the first English Statute Law to place certain restrictions upon the monarch. This meeting was later viewed as a prototype Parliament. Famous alumni of Merton Priory include Thomas Becket and Walter de Merton, who went on to establish Merton College at the University of Oxford.

In 1558, Henry VIII, using the powers of dissolution, shut down the Priory. Much of the Priory's stone and slate was removed to create the Royal Nonsuch Palace, located

7km to the south-west. The remaining foundations have been further damaged over the years, as a railway line, roads, pylons and factories have been built over the site. Only a precinct wall remains intact and located close to the banks of the Wandle (**1b**).

The line of the Roman road, Stane Street, running from London to Chichester, once ran through this site but it is also lost under centuries of industrialisation. The foundations of the Priory's Chapter House were recently unearthed when the nearby supermarket was being developed. These can be viewed

at the Merton Priory Visitor Centre (**1a**) beneath Merantun Way dual carriageway, every Sunday between the months of April and October.

2 Morris & Co Workshop William Morris was an English poet, writer, socialist, designer and advocate of the Art and Crafts movement. He founded the decorative arts company of Morris, Marshall, Faulkner & Co in 1861. Twenty years later, and with the company renamed as Morris & Co, he leased new workshops, the Merton Abbey Works, on the banks of the Wandle. The Works had previously been part of Merton Priory and a former Huguenot silk works. It was a relatively rural location, and close to Littler's Merton Abbey Mills just to the south (page 120), but the chalk stream waters were ideal for washing the finished fabrics. Morris's workshops occupied both sides of the river (the eastern side of the river is now covered by a Sainsbury's supermarket) and produced fabrics, stained glass, carpets and tapestries that became very popular with the Victorian middle and upper classes. The artist Edward Burne-Jones created numerous stained-glass windows for Morris & Co.

The fabrics were printed with organic dyes, as Morris had an aversion to modern chemical equivalents and of much else in

the industrialised world; he also rejected
mass-production methods, instead preferring
to employ craftsmen and women. The land
adjacent to the factory was used to grow
edible produce for the workers. However,
despite Morris's socialist leanings, the

workers were paid on a piecemeal basis
and offered no shares in the business. After
Morris's death in 1896, the workshops
continued operating until 1940. However,
the outbreak of the Second World War saw
the decline in the demand for luxury goods
and the buildings were demolished soon
afterwards.

In the post-war era the stampede

of industrialisation flattened just about
everything in the area. A cardboard
manufacturing plant and an engineering
factory were built here before a huge
supermarket was constructed over the site
to the east of the river. A wall belonging
to the Priory is still standing to the east of
Sainsbury's (**1b**).

3 Wandle Park

This park was once the
grounds of the Wandlebank House, home of
James Perry, editor of the *Morning Chronicle*,
who also owned the nearby Morton Mill.
The park is built upon what was once a mill
pond, which powered the Merton Corn
Mill. It became a public space in 1907, when
Wimbledon Corporation bought the estate
for £6,000.

In the 16th century the river was
straightened to maximise power for the mill,
with the original stream left to meander
around the eastern side of
what is now the park.

A settlement pond has
been created to avoid
flooding further downstream
and a short channel to the pond
has been placed to extract
pollutants by gravity from the
surface waterways, such as
rubber from tyres and litter.
These are then removed on
a regular basis. The reed and
watercress beds in the larger
pond extract other, smaller
pollutants.

*Clockwise from
left: a plan
of the former
Merton Priory;
the 13th century
seal of Merton
Priory; William
Morris standing
in front of a
wallpaper design
that was block
printed at the
Morris workshop
beside the River
Wandle.*

KEY

The route of the
former Roman road
Stane Street

I The Merton Mills The three-storey block of flats sited over the river was once the Merton Mills. Milling began here in the 13th century, possibly earlier. Over the centuries the mill wheels have been used to grind corn, hard wood for dyeing, and the fulling of cloth and leather. The current building was designed by John Rennie in the late 1790s. Rennie, a prolific engineer and architect, went on to design the first Waterloo Bridge in 1817.

James Perry (page 129), a major shareholder in the new horse-drawn railway, purchased the mills in 1804 and had a branch of the Surrey Iron Railway (page 128) brought to the mills to make the transportation of raw and finished material more efficient. The corn mill, with its seven pairs of grinding stones, was one of the largest in the county. In 1919, the Connolly Brothers bought the mill and converted it into a leather finishing operation. Much of the high-quality leather they produced was used in motor vehicles including for Rolls Royce. However, shortly after, they moved their operation to Kent, and the mill was converted into flats in 1994.

2 Wandle Meadow Nature Park

This verdant park was a sewage treatment works until the 1970s, and it wasn't until 1993 that the site was opened to the public. Despite the looming electricity pylons and railway line, the area has almost returned back to nature with a predominance of hazel, hawthorn, ash, silver birch trees and mature crack willows overhanging the Wandle.

Clockwise from the lower left: the Merton Mill with the river entrance to the former mill wheel; Wandle Meadow Nature Park; the viewing platform at the confluence of the rivers Wandle and Graveney as a kingfisher descends; the London Borough of Merton's logo which features a water wheel.

3 River Graveney A high-sided grey concrete revetment carries the River Graveney on its partial subterranean 5km journey from Tooting. Over the centuries this stream has been straightened and imprisoned within a human-made conduit. This was designed to help alleviate the threat of flooding. At the confluence with the Wandle is a viewing platform stretching over the two rivers.

4 Former watercress beds Until the early 20th century a large watercress bed sat on the eastern bank of the Wandle, where a carpet warehouse is now located. This was not an uncommon feature to be seen along this river.

5 AFC Wimbledon Just to the west of this path, on Plough Lane, is a series of modern six-storey apartments (**5a**). This was the home of Wimbledon FC until 1991. Following the Hillsborough Disaster in 1989, when 95 Liverpool supporters were killed due to a crowd crush, the Taylor Report recommended all-seater stadiums for the then First Division teams. It was difficult to adapt Wimbledon's stadium, Plough Lane, so they ground-shared with nearby Selhurst Park, home of Crystal Palace FC. The club spent ten years seeking a new home stadium in south London but were unsuccessful, so in 2001, they decided to relocate to Milton Keynes in Buckinghamshire and renamed the club MK Dons, which was not a popular outcome among fans, many of whom supported the creation of a new club, AFC Wimbledon, in 2002. The club initially ground-shared with other local teams until the new stadium was completed in 2020 (**5b**). The ground, also named Plough Lane, is sited upon the former Wimbledon Greyhound Stadium and is 200m away from the old ground.

1 Former Gunpowder Mill Close to the north end of Garratt Park, on Trewint Road, was a gunpowder mill that was established in the 1750s. Its usage was later changed to extracting oil from linseed. Like the Merton Mills (page 124), it was connected to the Surrey Iron Railway. By the 1860s, it had become a paper mill and finally a bone crushing facility before being destroyed by fire in 1890. A few of the mill out-buildings remain to the west of the river.

2 The Wandle splits As the Wandle enters Earlsfield, the river is split into two channels by a wall 300m in length. This area was once prone to flooding, so the river had to be made deeper to carry more water. In 1960, the work was carried out by the LCC. While this work was being done, the river still flowed, so a concrete wall, a cofferdam, was built along the middle of the stream. Once complete, the eastern side of the Wandle was sealed off at both ends and the water pumped out. Then the riverbed could be dug to a deeper level and a new concrete base added. Once the work was complete, the dams at each end were removed and the water flowed back in. The process would be then repeated on the western side of the river. However, removing the central cofferdam wall is difficult, and it may be needed again to clear the channels, so has been left in place.

3 King George's Park This park sits immediately to the south of Wandsworth

town centre and to the west of the Wandle and is nearly 1.5km of leisure, recreation and sports fields, created out of open fields and a rubbish tip in 1921. It was initially named Southfield's Park until it was formally opened by King George V in 1923.

Shortly after the Second World War, 100 prefabricated (prefab) houses were constructed on this section of the park (**3a**) as part of the solution to the housing crisis caused by wartime bombing. Although they were only intended to be occupied for ten years, this particular estate was used until the 1960s, when the land was reclaimed and turned back into playing fields. The River Wandle, as it enters Wandsworth, has since 1971 been culverted under the Southside Shopping Centre.

Huguenot Red Hat In the late 17th century, many French Protestant Huguenots fled France fearing religious persecution from the Roman Catholic regime. Several hundred Huguenots ended up in Wandsworth, bringing with them their skills of silk weaving and dyeing; south-west London was well away from the City of London Guilds, which could impose a restriction upon the numbers working in the business. The chalk stream of the Wandle was ideal for cleaning the red fabrics for which they had become famous. Red hats manufactured by the Huguenots in Wandsworth were ironically very popular with the Roman Catholic cardinals.

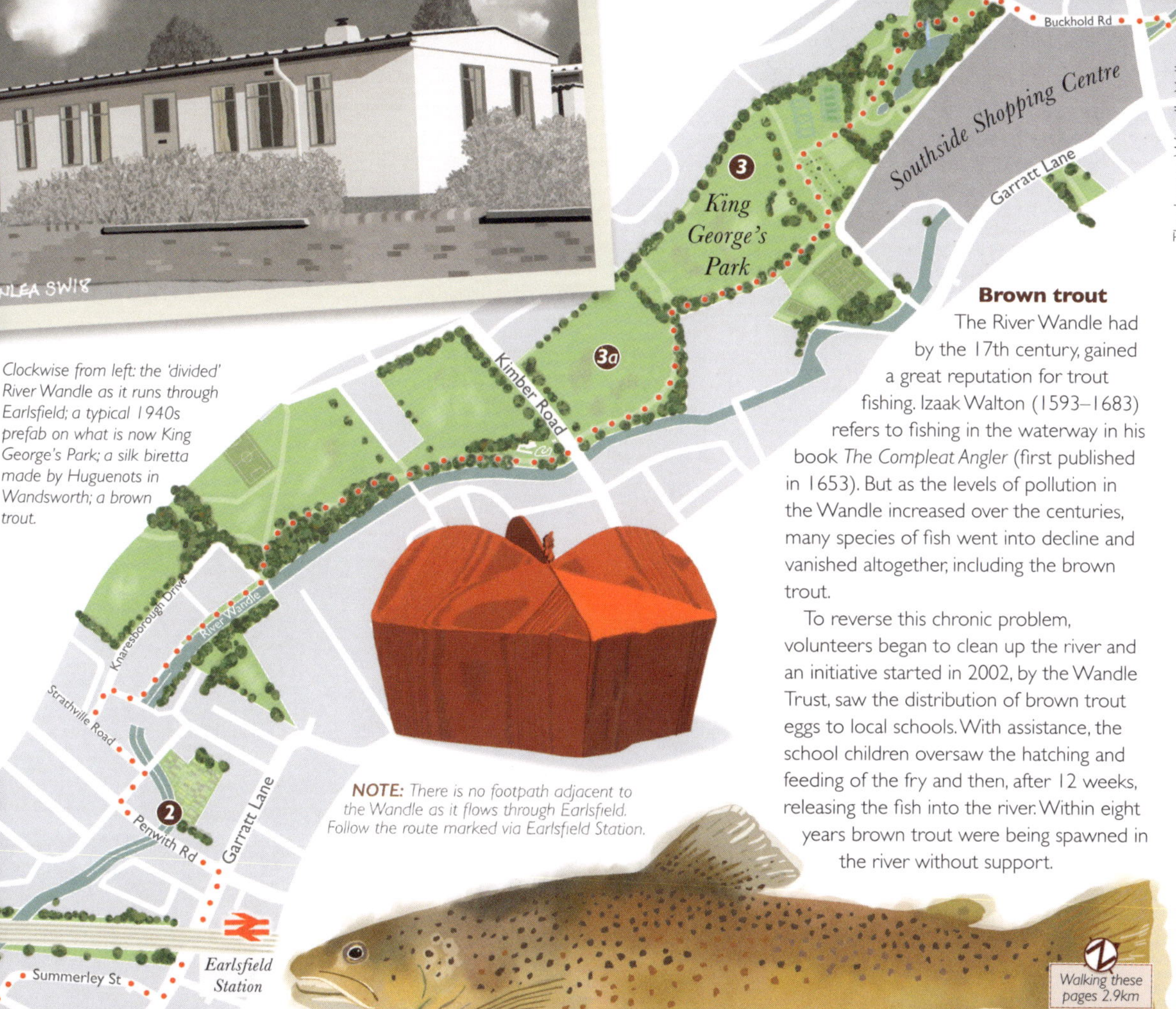

Clockwise from left: the 'divided' River Wandle as it runs through Earlsfield; a typical 1940s prefab on what is now King George's Park; a silk biretta made by Huguenots in Wandsworth; a brown trout.

NOTE: *There is no footpath adjacent to the Wandle as it flows through Earlsfield. Follow the route marked via Earlsfield Station.*

Brown trout

The River Wandle had by the 17th century, gained a great reputation for trout fishing. Izaak Walton (1593–1683) refers to fishing in the waterway in his book *The Compleat Angler* (first published in 1653). But as the levels of pollution in the Wandle increased over the centuries, many species of fish went into decline and vanished altogether, including the brown trout.

To reverse this chronic problem, volunteers began to clean up the river and an initiative started in 2002, by the Wandle Trust, saw the distribution of brown trout eggs to local schools. With assistance, the school children oversaw the hatching and feeding of the fry and then, after 12 weeks, releasing the fish into the river. Within eight years brown trout were being spawned in the river without support.

Wandsworth The south-west London town of Wandsworth was referred to in the Domesday Book of 1086 as Wandelesorde or Wendelsorde, although its location then was largely rural, on the banks of the Thames where one of its tributaries, the Wandle, fed in. The fast-flowing River Wandle, which powered many mill wheels, would establish the village as the oldest industrial zone in London and it became famous for its production of fabrics, paper and corn grinding.

In the 17th century, a group of Huguenot refugees settled in Wandsworth, attracted by the quality of the river water plus its energy for turning mill wheels. They introduced new techniques of silk production and methods of dying fabrics.

Wandsworth became renowned for its extensive brewing industry and being the home of the world's first public railway.

1 The Ram Brewery In 1581, the owners of the Ram Inn, Wandsworth, began brewing their own beer, and the process has continued at this location ever since. The Young family acquired the brewery in 1831 and began to expand the business.

The brewery's proximity to the River Thames was vital for getting materials in and finished produce out to the rest of the country and abroad. Water from the Wandle was used to cool the beer vats, and the canal created for the Surrey Iron Railway was extended into the brewery, though in 1930 this waterway was filled in to make way for a gas holder.

The Ram Brewery came to dominate Wandsworth town. And even in the late 20th century the sight of horse and drays delivering beer to local pubs was not unusual. In 2006, Young's moved the business to a modern processing site in Bedford. The Wandsworth site has been redeveloped into commercial and residential apartments and a micro-brewery has since been installed within one of the retained brewery buildings, thus maintaining the local tradition.

2 The Surrey Iron Railway Canal mania came late to London. The Grand Union Canal only reached Paddington in 1801. Around the same time a plan to build a canal alongside the Wandle had been proposed. However, this was vigorously opposed by the local mill owners, as it would draw water from the river and thus reduce power to the mills.

In 1799, engineer William Jessop recommended an iron railway, with trucks drawn by horses, which would run for 14km, along the banks of the Wandle between Wandsworth and Croydon. This idea was very well received by many local businessmen, including James Perry (page 124). The Act was passed in Parliament in 1801 and shares were sold.

The Surrey Iron Railway (SIR) was opened two years later and provided a service to a growing industry carrying coal, flour, beer, gunpowder, textiles and paper (*route of the railway track shown in the blue broken line on the map*). However, the advent of the steam railway resulted in the decline of the SIR and it closed down in 1846. A plaque commemorating the railway can be found in an alley leading to the Ram Quarter, just off Ram Street (**2a**).

3 The Causeway Just before it enters the Thames, the Wandle splits around an island called the Causeway. On the right-hand side of the road, before the railway bridge, is a sluice gate. Installed within it is a bell on which is inscribed 'I AM RUNG BY THE TIDES', since it used to sound the high and low waters twice daily. A turbine within the sluice formerly generated electricity for a nearby school and to ring the bell. Sadly, the turbine is no longer working. Immediately above the bell are the words 'Salmon, Swan, Otter, Heron, Eel', a tribute to the new life that has been restored to the River Wandle over the past few decades. At the northernmost tip of the Causeway, known as the Spit Nature Reserve, you can view the Wandle as it enters the Thames and the Fulham shore beyond.

4 Lower Mill Lower Mill once stood on what is now a bridge over the Wandle. Since the late 14th century there has been a flour mill at this location. It was demolished around 1900. This mill differed from all the other mills on the Wandle as it was powered by the rise and fall of the tides.

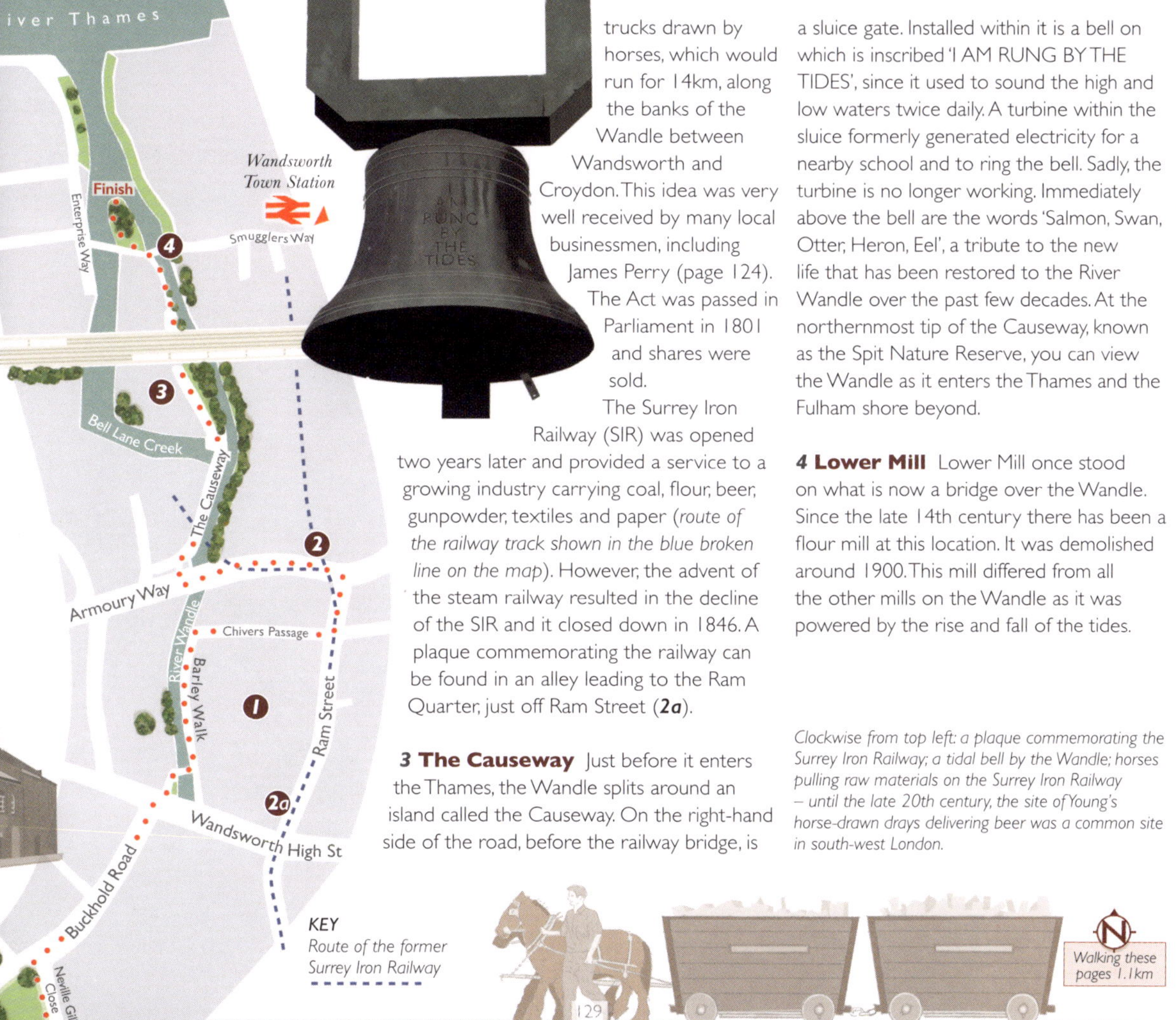

Clockwise from top left: a plaque commemorating the Surrey Iron Railway; a tidal bell by the Wandle; horses pulling raw materials on the Surrey Iron Railway – until the late 20th century, the site of Young's horse-drawn drays delivering beer was a common site in south-west London.

Opposite: deer in Richmond Park.

WIMBLEDON COMMON & PUTNEY HEATH

RICHMOND PARK – RICHMOND HILL

RICHMOND HILL – KINGSTON UPON THAMES

These three walks follow a trail through the largest common and park in London and along the verdant river path to Kingston upon Thames.

WIMBLEDON COMMON & PUTNEY HEATH

Total walking distance 12.2km

Wimbledon is probably best known for its lawn tennis championships, but it also has the largest common in the capital. And like so many of the other commons in London, its freedom from enclosure had to be fought for. Today, the Wimbledon and Putney Common boasts three golf clubs and many miles of footpaths and bridalways.

1 Wimbledon The village of Wimbledon, situated upon a hill south-west of London, was once one of several small settlements circling the largest open space, or Common, in the capital. Prior to the 19th century the edges of the Common were dotted with fine mansions belonging to wealthy owners.

The arrival of the railway below Wimbledon Hill, in 1838, allowed many middle-class people to move out of central London, away from the increasing industrial pollution to the cleaner air of Wimbledon. An infrastructure of domestic workers, gardeners, services and retail facilities followed, and they too needed to be housed within the area.

Today, Wimbledon, like so many other hilltop villages in the capital, retains a sense of affluence with its fine cafés, chic shops and expensive property. And, of course, the tennis championships have placed Wimbledon firmly on the international map.

2 Cannizaro Park

Cannizaro Park is a gem of an estate situated within the south-east corner of Wimbledon Common.

It was privately owned until 1949, however today it is managed by the London Borough of Merton and open to the public. The 14ha park contains many rare exotic trees and plants which have contributed towards its Grade II status.

Cannizaro House is now the Hotel du Vin. The building, first constructed in the early 1700s, was formerly known as Warren House, and was built for William Brown, a London merchant.

In the early 19th century, an Italian, Francis Plantamone, Count St Antonio, leased Warren House until 1832, when he left his wife, Sophia, to live with his mistress in Italy. The Count later inherited the title Duke of Cannizzaro in Sicily. And Sophia, despite the separation, took the title of Duchess of Cannizzaro. By the time of her death in 1841, the house was named after her title, though one 'z' was dropped from the name. A fire destroyed most of the structure in 1900 but it was soon rebuilt in a neo-Georgian style. During the First World War, however, the building fell into disrepair, but the arrival of new owners, Kenneth and Adela Wilson, in 1920 restored the fortunes of the estate. They planted many rare trees to complement those already in existence including black walnut, handkerchief and Persian ironwood. Many of the camellia, azaleas and rhododendrons the Wilson's planted are still visible today.

Not long after, the house was acquired by the council and was converted into a retirement home. In 1987, the building was sold and repurposed as a hotel.

3 Josephine Butler

In 1864, the Contagious Diseases Act was introduced in a bid to decrease venereal disease prevalence, especially in the armed forces. Police forces close to military bases were given powers to apprehend any woman they thought was a sex worker and subject them to an invasive medical inspection. The Act is believed to have forced some women into prostitution once their reputation had been diminished simply for being accused of sex work.

The feminist campaigner and social reformer Josephine Butler (1828–1906; see above) spent many years campaigning for the repeal of the demeaning Act. She described the examination as 'surgical or steel rape'. Thanks to her formidable activism, the Act was eventually repealed in 1886. A year later the age of consent was raised to 16, as it became apparent that girls as young as 13 were being forced to work as child prostitutes. Butler, a prolific writer of books and pamphlets, was also active in the struggle for women's votes and better education. She lived at 8 North View in the latter years of her life.

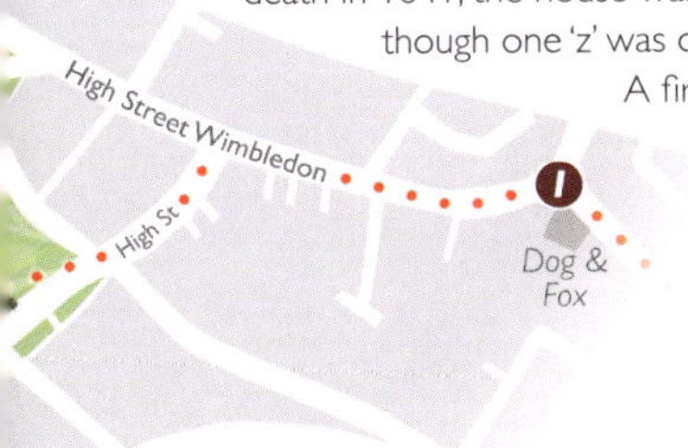

4 Sir Ernest Chain

German born biochemist, Ernest Chain (1906–1979) carried out research into the therapeutic action of penicillin at Oxford University, along with Howard Florey. In 1945, the pair, along with Alexander Fleming, were awarded the Nobel Prize for Medicine for this groundbreaking work. Chain lived at 9 North View and was knighted in 1969.

Clockwise from far left: Wimbledon Village, with the old fire station on the left-hand side; the Aviary in Cannizaro Park (it was modelled on Turin Cathedral); Josephine Butler and the Millennium Fountain, created by the sculptor Richard Rome.

Walking these pages 4.5km

1 Drinking fountain, cattle trough and pound This small animal pound

was probably used by bailiffs to hold confiscated farm animals (sheep and pigs) whose grazing rights upon the Common had expired. Just north of the pound is a fountain and animal trough, a gift of the MP Robert Hanbury. During redevelopment work in 1904, the animals were removed from their original location near St Mary-le-Strand, central London, and situated on Parkside, close to the MP's former residence and next to a cattle trough. The fountain is no longer working.

2 The Toynbee Family Joseph

Toynbee (1815–1866) was a renowned pioneering otologist and aural surgeon who practised at St Mary's Hospital in Paddington. He lived at 49 Parkside with his wife, Harriet, and their nine children. Joseph died in 1866 as a consequence of conducting experiments upon himself to cure tinnitus using chloroform and hydrogen cyanide.

One of Joseph and Harriet's sons, Arnold Toynbee (1852–1883), lived here as a child from the age of 2 to 14. He later studied political economy at Oxford. Through his research he dismissed the opinion that free trade was beneficial to all, especially the labourers. He was also an advocate of trade unions and state intervention. It is believed that Arnold introduced the phrase 'Industrial Revolution' into the English language, and he worked in the East End of London to establish libraries and education centres for the working classes. Unfortunately, in 1883, he died at the age of 30 due to overwork. The following year, Samuel and Henrietta Barnett established a non-sectarian permanent education centre in Whitechapel for the benefit of working-class people. It was named Toynbee Hall after Arnold Toynbee.

An English Heritage plaque on the house at 49 Parkside is dedicated to the father and son, Joseph and Arnold Toynbee. However, it does omit Grace Toynbee (1859–1946), the youngest daughter of Joseph and Harriet. Grace went on to become a microbiologist and was one of 19 signatories who petitioned in 1904 for women to be allowed into the Chemical Society (later the Royal Society of Chemistry).

3 Wimbledon Windmill Museum

In 1817, Charles March successfully applied for permission to construct a windmill on Wimbledon Common for the use and convenience of local corn growers. One of the conditions of the lease was that the miller had to act as a lookout for criminals and duellers.

When the Lord of the Manor began his campaign in 1865 to enclose the Common, he refused to extend the lease of the windmill. Following the preservation of the Common, the windmill and the adjacent Mill House were converted into accommodation for six families. Without doubt the most famous resident was Lord Robert Baden-Powell (1857–1941), founder of the Boy Scout movement. It was here, in this quiet, almost rural location that he wrote his famous book *Scouting for Boys*, in 1908. The building is now a museum of windmills with working models.

Clockwise from left: the animal pound on Parkside; father and son, Joseph and Arnold Toynbee; the former working windmill, now the Wimbledon Windmill Museum.

4 Wimbledon Common and Putney Heath At 445ha this is the largest heathland in London. Trees such as oaks, rowans, sweet chestnuts and maples are prolific on the Common and in medieval times local inhabitants were allowed to pollard trees for fuel. They could also graze cattle and dig for turf and gravel, but only between Michaelmas and the following April. From the 16th century the Common was used for military target practice and manoeuvres. The National Rifle Association began shooting competitions on the Common in 1860, until the range of the rifle became too great and they had to move to a safer area.

When Earl Spencer, Lord of the Manor of Mortlake, attempted to enclose the Common in 1865 with a Private Bill in Parliament, he met with massive resistance from the newly established middle classes, who were beginning to create and occupy comfortable homes bordering the land. The arrival of the railways enabled many wealthy Londoners to escape the ailments and toxic smells that were enveloping the industrialised capital in the 1840s and 50s. The Wimbledon Common Committee was formed, and legal resistance was offered. In 1870, Earl Spencer finally backed down and ownership of the Common passed to the trustees with a levy being collected annually for the upkeep of the space from those living within just over a kilometre of the Common. Today the Common is a much-valued asset for all those seeking exercise and fresh air within a huge green space.

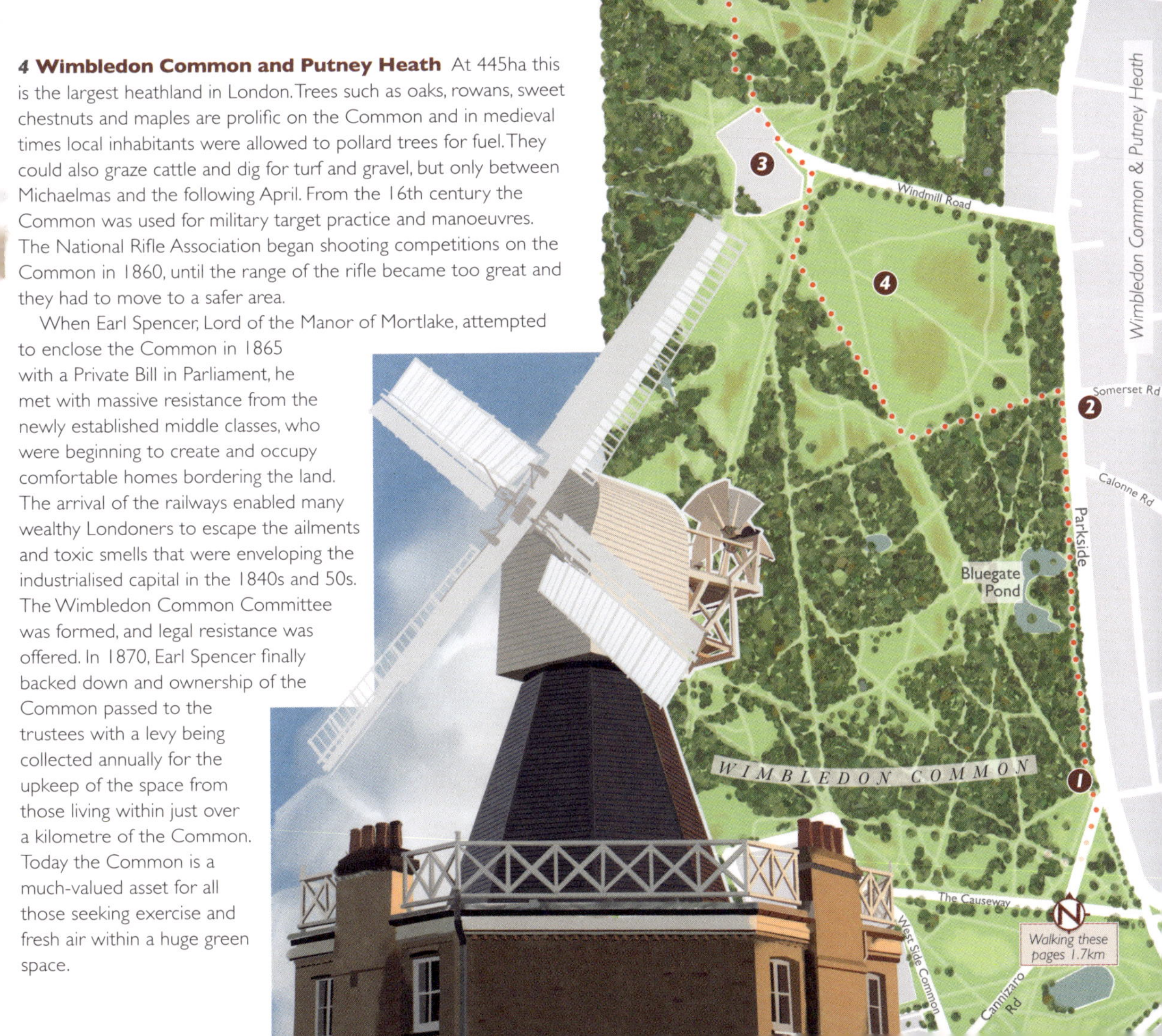

1 Jerry's Hill The hill that was named after Jerry all sounds quite innocuous. But it was far from the case. Jeremiah 'Jerry' Abershawe was a 22-year-old highwayman, who was caught, tried and hung on Kennington Common in 1795 for his misdemeanours. His body was placed in a gibbet and displayed at this spot close to the highway (now the A3) for several years as a deterrent to other would-be criminals. Abershawe was the last highwayman in England to be displayed in such a gruesome manner. In 1798, Prime Minister William Pitt the Younger fought a duel with William Tierney MP very close to the gibbet. Both men paced out their 12 steps, turned to shoot and missed each other.

2 Golf on the Common

Wimbledon Common is home to two golf courses and three clubs: London Scottish Golf Club (LSGC), Royal Wimbledon Golf Club (RWGC) and Wimbledon Common Golf Club (WCGC).

The LSGC was founded following a shooting competition on the Common in 1864. The London Scottish Rifle Volunteers met and agreed to prepare a seven-hole golf course. The following year, golf was played for the first time on the Common. Six years later the

course was extended to 18 holes. The former Victorian club house is now the Wimbledon Windmill Museum.

A disagreement between the military and non-military members of the LSGC in 1881 led to a civilian group establishing the RWGC. By 1907, they had created their own golf course to the south, with its club house on Camp Road. The following year, the WCGC was formed and began to share the course with the LSGC. This arrangement continues to this day, although they now have separate club houses. The LSGC and WCGC golf course is part of the open Common, and golfers are asked to be aware of walkers and horse riders crossing the fairways. A local byelaw insists that all players must wear pillar-box red tops. The RWGC plays on a fenced-off section of the Common.

3 Caesar's Well Wimbledon Common is largely gravel overlaying London Clay. As rainwater filters through the gravel and reaches the impervious clay, it results in springs appearing above ground. Several springs are to be found on the Common and were often used as a source of water. This particular spring was named after the nearby Caesar's Camp. The inscription within the shallow well reads 'HW Peek MP 1872' and is a reference to Henry W Peek, the local MP who headed the committee to save the Common from being enclosed. The spring dried up in 1911 but another later formed a few metres away, its waters flowing down into the Beverley Brook.

4 Caesar's Camp Despite Roman pottery being discovered here and the name of the location, there is no evidence that any Roman Caesar ever visited. However, there is evidence that this was once a late Iron Age (700 BC) fort, roughly 300m in diameter and complete with a defensive ditch. Sadly, the ramparts were largely demolished in 1875 by two Victorian property developers. Much of the former camp sits within the golf course. A plaque marks the site *(on the map: a circular white tint denotes perimeter of the former camp)*.

5 Beverley Brook This 14.5km-long stream rises near Worcester Park and heads north, where it flanks the western border of Wimbledon Common before heading into Richmond Park and finally the River Thames opposite Craven Cottage, the home of Fulham FC. Like its eastern neighbour, the River Wandle, it was not culverted. The river's name is derived from the beavers that used to swim in the watercourse that passed through the meadow or ley. The European beaver has been extinct from Britain for over 400 years (though they are gradually being reintroduced).

Clockwise from left: a red-topped golfer tees off at the Wimbledon Common Golf Club; Caesar's Well; a sign featuring the highwayman 'Jerry' Abershaw at nearby Tibbets Corner on the A3.

RICHMOND PARK – RICHMOND HILL

Total walking distance 11.2km

At just over 1,000ha, Richmond Park is the largest piece of open land in London, and is home to a variety of 130,000 trees. The park receives 5.5 million visitors per year, many of whom are here to walk and experience the remoteness that such a vast space has to offer. Others come to this Royal Park to cycle, play golf, fish or horse ride.

1 Richmond Park The English royals have, until the past few hundred years, opted for palaces along the River Thames. The river offered a secure and quick mode of travel between regal abodes, as unmetalled road surfaces, surrounded by forests, were considered unsafe even if travelling with mounted guards.

In 1497, Henry VII rebuilt a manor house here in an area known as Shene (a district to the east is still known as Sheen). Henry

renamed the new palace, close to the Thames *(below left)* Richmond, after his earldom in Richmond, North Yorkshire. Henry VIII was born here and from an early age developed a love of hunting in the forests and green space nearby.

In 1625, a plague began to sweep through London. It was the first year of Charles I reign and he opted to move out of his Whitehall palace and head to Richmond for safety. The epidemic would kill 40,000 Londoners. While in Richmond, the monarch planned a deer park to the south-east of the palace on a massive piece of land that would become known as Richmond Park.

While the monarch enjoyed deer hunting on Richmond Park, he did not want commoners accessing the land. So, in 1637, he ordered the enclosure of the hunting ground with a 13km-long brick wall. Although six access gates were installed, the enclosure was unpopular with locals who were used to wandering the park, and with several of the landowners, who owned sections of the enclosed estate. Few tears were shed by those local to the park when Charles I was beheaded in 1649 during the English Civil War, and the park fell into the ownership of the Commonwealth.

After the Civil War, park ownership was restored to the monarchy with the wall still in place, and local resentment grew. In 1751, Princess Amelia, daughter of George II, became the ranger of Richmond Park, and

having learned nothing from Charles I, she decided to make the park accessible only to her friends and the gates were sealed up. Four years later, a local brewer, John Lewis, decided to test the right-of-way in court. Though it took Lewis three years to fight the restriction, he eventually won, and the stile-gates were reinstalled.

2 White Lodge This fine example of early Palladian Revival was completed in 1729 and became a hunting lodge for George II. In 1813, Viscount Sidmouth, Henry Addington (prime minister from 1801 to 1804) was appointed deputy ranger of Richmond Park. The job of ranger or deputy ranger carried great responsibility; this task was usually bestowed by the monarch to a minor royal or a prime

minister. Addington was also given the White Lodge as a grace and favour residence. The former prime minister made several improvements to the park by adding a new plantation at nearby Spankers Hill with oak, larch, spruce and sweet chestnuts.

The future King Edward VIII was born at White Lodge in 1887. Since 1955, it has been home to younger dance students of the Royal Ballet School.

3 Pen Ponds These two sizable human-made ponds at the very heart of Richmond Park cover 9ha. They are probably so named as they were once sheep or deer pens before the stream, a tributary of the Beverley Brook, was dammed in 1746 to form these two pools. The ponds were drained during the Second World War as they acted as a navigation aid for enemy bombers. Today, they are a good place to view water birds. Fishing in the well-stocked ponds is permitted, though only with a licence.

Clockwise from left: the location of the former Richmond Palace in relation to the River Thames and Richmond Park; White Lodge; a view along the causeway between the Pen Ponds.

1 Isabella Plantation This fenced-off 17ha 'park within a park', was created by Lord Sidmouth (page 138) in 1831, during his term as deputy ranger of Richmond Park. The enclosure was essential to keep the deer from feeding on the new trees and plants. The majority of trees within the plantation are sweet chestnuts, oaks and beech.

The park did not open to the public until 1953, but today the plantation is renowned, particularly in spring, for its displays of acers, azaleas, rhododendrons and especially the Japanese Kurume azaleas. No such bushes are present elsewhere within the park as the deer would munch them all.

It would be easy to assume that the Isabella Plantation was named after a royal princess. However, it is more likely to be a corruption of the word 'isabel', meaning dingy or greyish yellow, a description the colour of the soil in the area. The term 'isabelline' still exists in the naming of animal and bird colours.

2 Pembroke Lodge This house once had the intriguing title of Molecatcher's Cottage. In 1788, the lodge was redesigned by Sir John Soane (the Neo-Classic architect, would later go on the design the Bank of England). In 1847, Queen Victoria granted permission for her prime minister Lord John Russell to live at Pembroke Lodge for the rest of his life. Russell's grandson, the future philosopher and mathematician Bertrand Russell, was orphaned at the age of three and was moved into Pembroke Lodge, which became home until he completed his degree at Cambridge. During the Second World War the house was used by the GHQ Liaison Regiment, a military intelligence unit. Today, the house is a restaurant and a wedding venue. At the highest point on Richmond Park, it offers great views of the Thames.

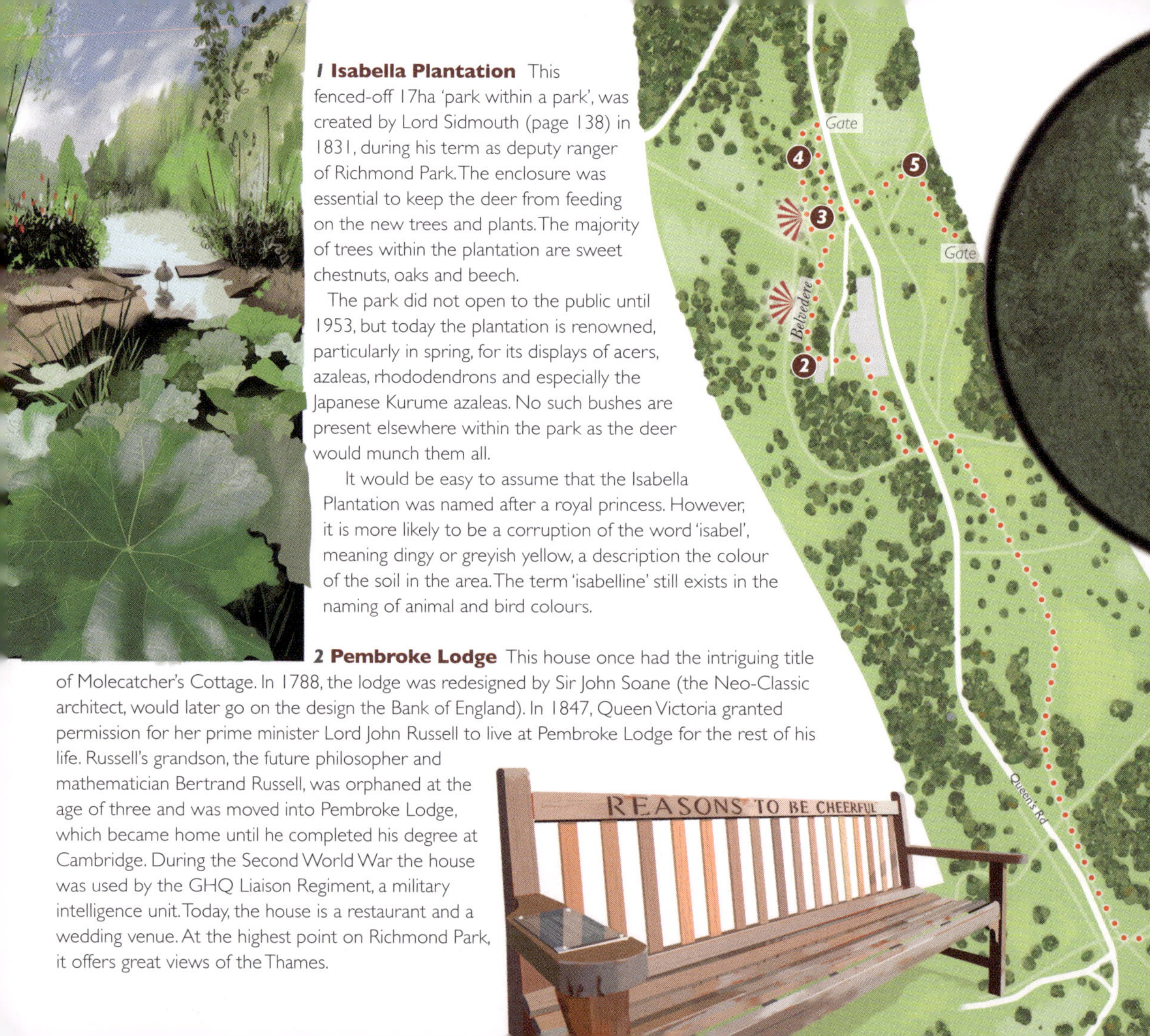

3 King Henry's Mound The mound (52m high) is believed to be a Bronze Age burial chamber. There is also a tale that Henry VIII stood on this hill and watched a rocket being launched from the Tower of London (17km away) in May 1536. The flare was to indicate that Anne Boleyn had been executed and that he could marry Jane Seymour. Sadly, there is nothing to substantiate this story.

On a fine day the views from the mound are spectacular. To the west, Ham House, Strawberry Hill, Eel Pie Island and Windsor Castle are visible. And to the east the 'protected view' of St Paul's Cathedral can be seen through a cutting in the trees. A telescope has been installed to assist with this observation.

4 Ian Dury's memorial bench In an area just to the north of King Henry's Mound is Poet's Corner. Within this space is a bench in memory of the new wave singer-songwriter and actor Ian Dury. At an early age, Dury was diagnosed with polio. In 1977, he formed the band Ian Dury and the Blockheads and their first single 'Sex & Drugs & Rock & Roll' was banned by the BBC. Regardless, the band went on to have huge success. Dury died of cancer in 2000, aged 57.

Inscribed onto the bench are the words from one of the Blockhead songs 'Reasons to Be Cheerful'. The bench also features a QR code, which visitors can scan on a smartphone to listen to Dury's music and an interview with him.

5 'The Way' These ornate metal gates, entitled 'The Way', were designed and made by the blacksmith Joshua De Lisle to mark the tercentenary of St Paul's Cathedral in 2011. The dome of St Paul's, 15km away, is visible on a good day through a clearing in the trees. The gates, adorned with metallic oak leaves and a wren, represent both the nearby trees and the architect of St Paul's, Sir Christopher Wren.

Clockwise from top left: Peg's Pond within the Isabella Plantation; a telescope view of St Paul's Cathedral from King Henry's Mound; 'The Way' gates; Ian Dury's memorial bench in Poet's Corner.

Walking these pages 3.7km

1 The ancient Royal Oak This ancient oak is estimated to be 750 years old and was a mere sapling when Edward I (1272–1307) was on the throne. It is located between Sidmouth Wood and the Queen Elizabeth's Plantation and is referred to as one of London's great trees.

Of the 130,000 trees within Richmond Park, there are around 1,200 ancient trees (those over 500 years old). Many of the most mature trees are to be found around the southern section of the park close to Kingston Gate, including hornbeam, hawthorns and sweet chestnuts. A feature of many trees within Richmond Park is that the boughs rarely hang lower than 1.5m from the ground as the deer nibble the new shoots.

2 Richmond Park deer Charles I introduced a herd of around 2,000 deer to Richmond Park in 1637 for the purposes of hunting. He also had a 13km brick wall constructed to prevent the deer from straying. It is the deer herds that shaped the park we see today. They eat new tree saplings (unless they are protected), which in turn has created several wide open spaces and fashioned a 'browse line' of 1.5m from the ground, where they eat the leaves and twigs.

Today, around 630 red and fallow deer occupy the park. Every November the deer population has to be culled to keep the numbers at a manageable level. The venison was formerly destined for the tables of the monarchy and their entourage, but today it is sold off through meat dealers and the profits used for the upkeep of the animals. Visitors are advised, for their own safety, to keep at least a 50m distance from the wild deer herds.

3 Royal Star and Garter Home Just outside the Richmond Gates is the huge brick and stone construction known as the Royal Star and Garter Home. The south-west-facing gardens to the rear have commanding views along the River Thames. A hotel once stood on this site during the Victorian era and during the First World War it was designated as a refuge for young soldiers with disabilities. Following the war, the establishment was rebuilt and continued to be used in this way until 2011. By the beginning of the 21st century, facilities at the Royal Star and Garter Home were not favourable for the care of elderly patients, so the building was sold and the residents moved to state-of-the-art facilities elsewhere. In 2014, the building was sold and converted into expensive residential apartments.

4 Terrace Gardens These public gardens, opened in 1887, are an amalgamation of several former private grounds. The sloping, well-managed gardens offer fantastic views over the River Thames and the only view in England protected by an Act of Parliament. Terrace Gardens is connected to Buccleuch Gardens by a flint-lined barrel-vaulted tunnel, known as the Grotto Gate (**4a**), which runs under Petersham Road.

5 Spring Well At the beginning of the 18th century people began to travel to this spa to 'take the waters'. The water, rich in magnesium sulphate (Epsom salts), was imbibed for health reasons. Richmond Spa, as it became known, developed a reputation, and a house was erected nearby to serve the efficacious water and provide other entertainment such as dining and dancing. The spa closed in 1780 and today a rusty old gate marks the entrance to the well.

6 Old Father Thames This statue of the reclining river god Old Father Thames was acquired by the Duke of Montagu in 1781 for display in his gardens at Buccleuch House (very close to this point). The statue, cast in Coade stone (an artificial material), has been damaged over the years. In 1992, it was restored and relocated to Terrace Gardens where Old Father Thames keep a watchful eye on the river below. Another copy can be found in Ham House (page 145).

Left to right: a statue of Old Father Thames in Terrace Gardens; the ancient Royal Oak, estimated to be 750 years old, now protected by a wooden fence; deer in Richmond Park.

RICHMOND HILL – KINGSTON UPON THAMES

Total walking distance 7.2km

Along this verdant walk upon the banks of the Thames, you will see many fine houses; an island where, it is claimed, the Swinging Sixties began, the largest lock and weir on the Thames; and several prosperous towns, one of which witnessed the coronation of seven kings. This is also a landscape that inspired many reknowned artists.

1 Buccleuch Gardens This narrow strip of grass and trees overlooking the Thames was once part of the old Buccleuch House private estate. In 1887, the grounds fell into public ownership along with the adjacent Terrace Gardens. The grounds can be accessed from Terrace Gardens via the Grotto Gate tunnel under Petersham Road. Buccleuch House no longer stands.

2 Petersham Meadows Cattle have grazed on these meadows for many centuries. The waterside land was once part of the Ham House estate (**5**) until it was sold off in the late 19th century. Not long after this, a plan was devised to create a housing estate here, but locals campaigned vigorously to stop the scheme and preserve the view from Richmond Hill. An Act of Parliament was passed in 1902 to ensure the vista was permanently saved. The lower section of the meadow is susceptible to flooding.

3 Marble Hill House George II had this fine Palladian villa built for his mistress, Henrietta Howard. It was set upon land sloping down to the Thames and completed in 1729. Henrietta was at the time married to the brutish and alcoholic Charles Howard, 9th Earl of Suffolk. They both held posts within the royal household, so Marble Hill House, at least 25km away from London by boat, seemed like a safe haven away from her husband and also acted as a place to entertain the king. She later became friends with Prime Minister Horace Walpole and the poet Alexander Pope, both of whom lived nearby. Henrietta was one of the few women at the time to own property.

Towards the end of the 18th century the house was home to Maria Fitzherbert, who had illegally married the Prince of Wales, later George VI, in 1785. Their marriage was declared void and he was obliged to marry Caroline of Brunswick (page 96), though he continued his affair with Fitzherbert at Marble House. The property fell into dereliction in the latter part of the 19th century but was saved in 1902 when the London County Council bought it for £40,000. Today, the house is managed by English Heritage.

4 Hammerton's Ferry Until 1729, there were only two bridges crossing the Thames between the City of London and Kingston. To cross the river elsewhere required a ferry, and these were plentiful along the river. Hammerton's Ferry, founded by Walter Hammerton, became operational in 1908 following the opening of Marble Hill House to the public and the introduction of a public footpath on the Surrey shore. Despite a legal challenge from the owners of the Twickenham Ferry in 1913, the ferry is still conveying pedestrians and cyclists between the two shores today. The ferry

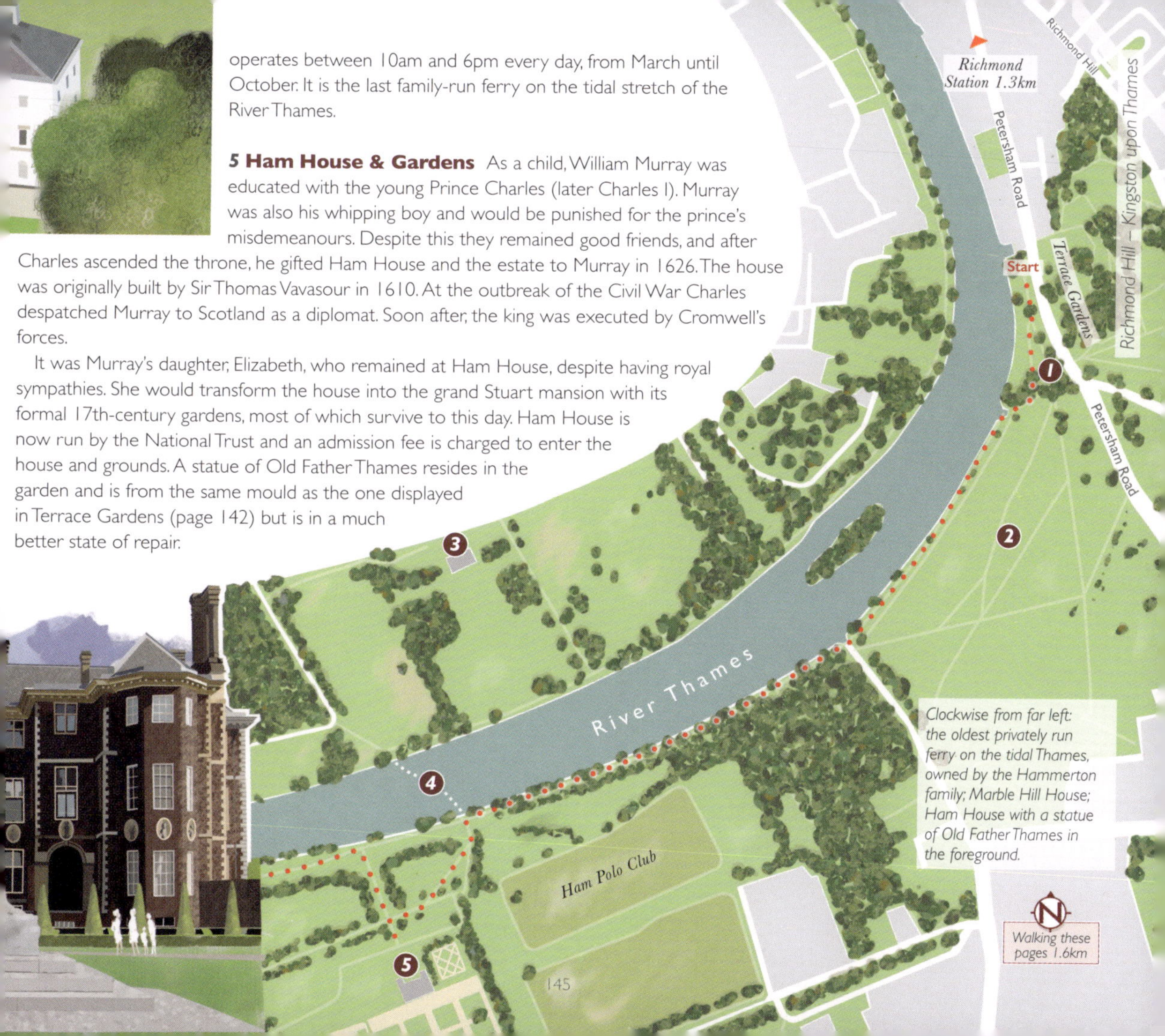

operates between 10am and 6pm every day, from March until October. It is the last family-run ferry on the tidal stretch of the River Thames.

5 Ham House & Gardens As a child, William Murray was educated with the young Prince Charles (later Charles I). Murray was also his whipping boy and would be punished for the prince's misdemeanours. Despite this they remained good friends, and after Charles ascended the throne, he gifted Ham House and the estate to Murray in 1626. The house was originally built by Sir Thomas Vavasour in 1610. At the outbreak of the Civil War Charles despatched Murray to Scotland as a diplomat. Soon after, the king was executed by Cromwell's forces.

It was Murray's daughter, Elizabeth, who remained at Ham House, despite having royal sympathies. She would transform the house into the grand Stuart mansion with its formal 17th-century gardens, most of which survive to this day. Ham House is now run by the National Trust and an admission fee is charged to enter the house and grounds. A statue of Old Father Thames resides in the garden and is from the same mould as the one displayed in Terrace Gardens (page 142) but is in a much better state of repair.

Clockwise from far left: the oldest privately run ferry on the tidal Thames, owned by the Hammerton family; Marble Hill House; Ham House with a statue of Old Father Thames in the foreground.

1 Eel Pie Island This 570m-long island was formerly named Twickenham Ait (an Old English word for eyot or island, often found on the Thames). However, it is today better known as Eel Pie Island after the tavern located here became famous for serving the pastry dish to Victorian day-trippers travelling down from London by steamboat. It is said that Henry VII stopped here to sample the pies en route to Windsor Castle.

In the 1960s, the island gained notoriety as a music venue, when many fledgling bands, including The Rolling Stones, Pink Floyd and The Who, played in the Eel Pie Island Hotel, leading to the claim of this being a cradle of British rock music. The bands' roadies had to carry all their equipment and instruments over the narrow footbridge. It closed in 1967 when the owners refused to update the building to comply with fire regulations. It was then occupied by squatters and destroyed by fire in 1971.

Today, the island is a mixture of expensive homes, studios and boatbuilding yards. It is closed to the public except for a few days each year.

During a very dry summer in 1884, it became possible to play cricket on the riverbed between the island and the Twickenham bank. The construction of a weir at Richmond in 1894 prevented this from ever occurring again.

2 Twickenham Mention Twickenham today and most people will think of the Twickenham Stadium, home of Rugby Football Union. Long before an oval ball had been kicked in this area, an Anglo-Saxon village, known as Twica – a term that described a split in the river around Eel Pie Island – was established.

By the 18th century the village, centred on St Mary's Church, had become popular with many famous and wealthy people who came to escape the increasing stink and pestilence of the capital. The arrival of the railway in 1848 and the facility to commute to London made Twickenham an even more attractive option. This is still the case today, and the district is an affluent area in which to live and work.

3 Ham Lands The flood meadow was once part of the Earl of Dysart's Ham House estate. In the early 20th century the southern

146

section of Ham Lands was leased by Ham River Grit Company to excavate gravel and sand for use in the construction business, with much of the material being shipped out by barges along the Thames. Most of the pits were later filled in once exhausted of the raw materials.

4 Pope's Grotto On the opposite shore, viewed through the trees, is an imposing two-storey neo-Tudor structure with a clock tower built in 1845 for Thomas Young, a tea merchant. Today it is an independent school, but the grounds were once the site of Alexander Pope's house. The poet and satirist (1688–1744) had lived close to the River Thames at various locations all his life. In 1719, following his successful translation of Homer's *The Iliad* he commissioned a house of Palladian style to be constructed on the banks of the river in Twickenham. He later commissioned a tunnel, lined with various geological specimens, mirrors, statues and shells, connected to the basement. Pope would retreat into these chambers to find inspiration in the gloom and damp. He continued to live in the house until his death in 1744 and is buried in the nearby church of St Mary's. The house was later demolished and replaced, however Pope's Grotto, now Grade II* listed, has largely survived and is open to visitors on certain weekends of the year.

5 Thames Young Mariners This 4ha lagoon, formerly a gravel pit, is connected to the Thames by a lock. The facility offers water and land-based activities for school-age children, including sailing, canoeing, kayaking, mountain biking, camping, archery and woodland skills.

Left to right: Eel Pie Island – an isle of boatbuilders, workshops and riverside dwellers; inside the South Chamber of Pope's Grotto; canoeists on the water at the Thames Young Mariners facility; a 1968 Eel Pie Island events poster.

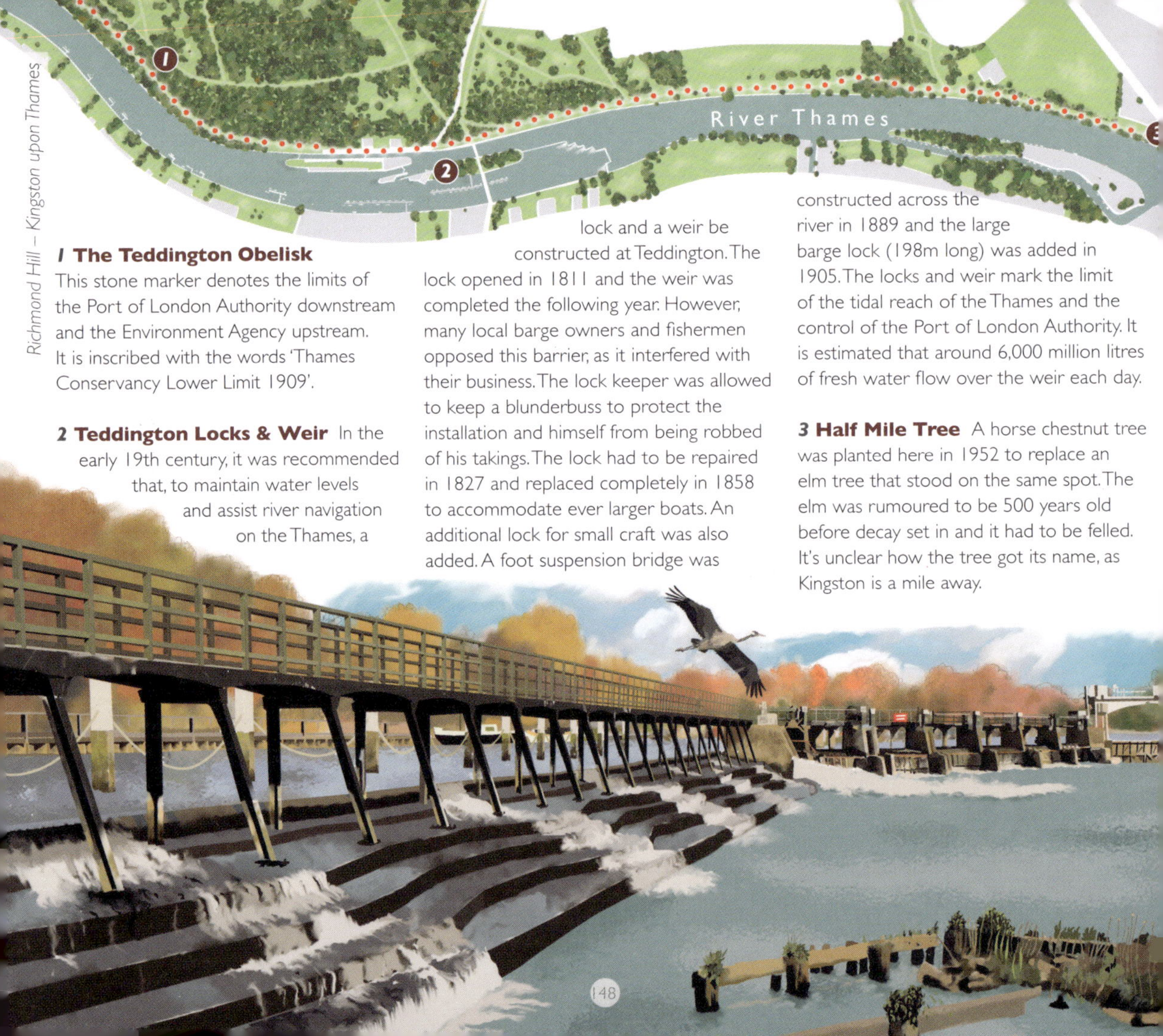

1 The Teddington Obelisk

This stone marker denotes the limits of the Port of London Authority downstream and the Environment Agency upstream. It is inscribed with the words 'Thames Conservancy Lower Limit 1909'.

2 Teddington Locks & Weir

In the early 19th century, it was recommended that, to maintain water levels and assist river navigation on the Thames, a lock and a weir be constructed at Teddington. The lock opened in 1811 and the weir was completed the following year. However, many local barge owners and fishermen opposed this barrier, as it interfered with their business. The lock keeper was allowed to keep a blunderbuss to protect the installation and himself from being robbed of his takings. The lock had to be repaired in 1827 and replaced completely in 1858 to accommodate ever larger boats. An additional lock for small craft was also added. A foot suspension bridge was constructed across the river in 1889 and the large barge lock (198m long) was added in 1905. The locks and weir mark the limit of the tidal reach of the Thames and the control of the Port of London Authority. It is estimated that around 6,000 million litres of fresh water flow over the weir each day.

3 Half Mile Tree

A horse chestnut tree was planted here in 1952 to replace an elm tree that stood on the same spot. The elm was rumoured to be 500 years old before decay set in and it had to be felled. It's unclear how the tree got its name, as Kingston is a mile away.

4 Kingston Bridge

Two thousand years ago the river was fordable here at low water and so became a vital strategic crossing point, and later, a series of wooden bridges were built across the river. Henry VIII considered the bridge of such importance that he paid for repairs and upgraded it to carry artillery over the Thames.

Until 1729, when Putney Bridge was built, Kingston was the first river crossing point after London Bridge. The tidal river (until 1812) caused much damage to the wooden bridge and it was constantly being repaired. In 1814, a heavy frost did further damage to the structure (this was the year of the last ice fair on the Thames in London). Finally, in 1825, following an Act of Parliament, a new stone crossing was commissioned, which opened three years later. The five arch bridge was constructed in Portland s-one and built 30m upstream of the old bridge. The bridge has twice been widened – in 1914 and 2000, to accommodate more traffic – with the stone façade being preserved. Remains of the old medieval bridge can still be seen in the basement of the John Lewis store.

5 Kingston upon Thames

This market town was granted Royal Borough status by King John in 1200 and is the oldest of the four such Boroughs. Three hundred years earlier the town was named Cyningestum, or the King's Estate, later Kingston. The town witnessed the coronation of seven Anglo-Saxon kings including Edward the Elder (son of Alfred) in AD 900 and Elthelred the Unready in AD 978. They were all crowned in St Mary Magdalen Church (now All Saints Church, **5a**) on a coronation stone that is now displayed outside the Guildhall (**5b**).

The market town status was enhanced when Charles I granted a charter that forbade other towns within an 11km radius from holding a market. The monarch was attempting to curry favour with many local landowners in order to create his new hunting grounds in Richmond Park (page 142). During the Civil War the town held key military status and was won and lost by both sides.

Kingston is the birthplace of photographer Eadweard Muybridge and author John Galsworthy, and the starting point of Jerome K Jerome's *Three Men in a Boat*. Today, it is a thriving shopping area, mainly pedestrianised with a popular market place.

Clockwise from above: Kingston Bridge; the Teddington Obelisk; the weir at Teddington.

Walking these pages 4.0km

ACKNOWLEDGEMENTS

My sincere thanks to all who have assisted in the creation this book, including: Beverley Charters and John Haggerty of the House Mill, Bromley-by-Bow ❖ Kenneth Greenway, Cemetery Park Manager, and Richard Nimmo, Cemetery Park Officer, of Tower Hamlets Cemetery Park ❖ Ian Shacklock, chair of the Friends of the Regent's Canal ❖ Stephen Llewellyn, treasurer of the Wandsworth Heritage ❖ Colin Davey, historian and guide ❖ And to those who have walked and checked several of the routes, including Florence Fathers, Sheila Fathers and Michael Court.

A special thank you to Hunter Davies for very kindly writing the foreword to this book.

Thanks also go to Elizabeth Multon, Jenny Clark and Kate Savage at Bloomsbury for assisting me with the production of this book and for allowing me the freedom to write, illustrate and design this book as I had originally envisaged.

And finally, once again, a huge thanks to my wife, Sheila Fathers, for her great assistance in proof-reading my sometimes dubious copy before it headed off to the publishers.

SELECTED BIBLIOGRAPHY

Ackroyd, Peter, *London The Biography*, Chatto & Windus 2000

Ackroyd, Peter, *Thames*, Vintage 2008

Barton, Nicholas & Myers, Stephen, *The Lost Rivers of London*, Historical Publications 2016

Beard, Geoffrey, *The Works of Christopher Wren*, Bloomsbury 1987

Brown, Matt, *Everything You Know About London Is Wrong*, Batsford 2016

Cameron-Cooper, Gilly, *Walking London's Docks, Rivers & Canals*, New Holland 2005

Chivers, Tom, *London Clay*, Doubleday 2021

Croad, Stephen, *Liquid History*, Batsford 2003

Davies, Caitlin, *Taking the Water*, Frances Lincoln 2012

Davies, Hunter, *The Heath*, Head of Zeus 2021

Davies, Hunter, *London Parks*, Simon & Schuster 2021

Fathers, David, *Bloody London*, Conway/Bloomsbury 2020

Fathers, David, *London's Hidden Rivers*, Frances Lincoln 2017

Faulkner, Alan, *The Regent's Canal*, Waterways World 2005

Gilbert, Bob, *The London Green Way*, Lawrence & Wishart 2012

Glinert, Ed, *The London Compendium*, Penguin 2012

Gwynn, Robin D, *Huguenot Heritage*, Routledge & Kegan Paul 1985

Hampshire, David, *London's Green Walks*, City Books 2018

Hatts, Leigh, *Walking the Lea Valley*, Cicerone 2015

Howard, Rachel & Nash, Bill, *Secret London*, Jonglez 2011

Matthews, Peter, *London's Bridges*, Shire Publications 2008

McDowall, David & Wolton, Deborah, *The Walker's Guide to Hampstead Heath*, David McDowall 2006

Meller, Hugh, *London Cemeteries*, Ashgate Publishing 1981

Millar, Stephen, *London's Hidden Walks*, Metro Publications 2014

Myers, Stephen, *Walking on Water*, Amberley Publishing 2011

Pevsner, Nikolaus & Cherry, Bridget, *London 2: South*, Yale University Press 2002

Pevsner, Nikolaus & Cherry, Bridget, *London 4: North*, Yale University Press 1994

Pevsner, Nikolaus, Cherry, Bridget & O'Brian Charles, *London 5: East*, Yale University Press 1994

Rabbits, Paul, *London's Royal Parks*, Shire Publications 2014

Richardson, John, *The Annals of London*, University of California 2000

Smith, Rob, *Industrial History of the Lower River Lea*, 2020

Steel, Bob & Coleman, Derek, *River Wandle Companion*, Culverhouse Books 2012

Sunderland, Septimus, *Old London's Spas, Baths & Wells*, John Bale, Sons & Danielsson 1915

Weinreb, Ben & Hibbert, Christopher, *The London Encyclopaedia*, Macmillan 1983

Winn, Christopher, *I Never Knew That About London*, Ebury Press 2007

Wood, Paul, *London Is a Forest*, Quadrille 2019

Wood, Paul, *Great Trees of London Map*, Blue Crow Media 2020

SELECTED WEBSITES

google.co.uk/maps

layersoflondon.org

openstreetmap.org

royalparks.org.uk

PICTURE CREDITS

Lordship Lane Station by Emile Pissarrio (page 111)

Also by *David Fathers*

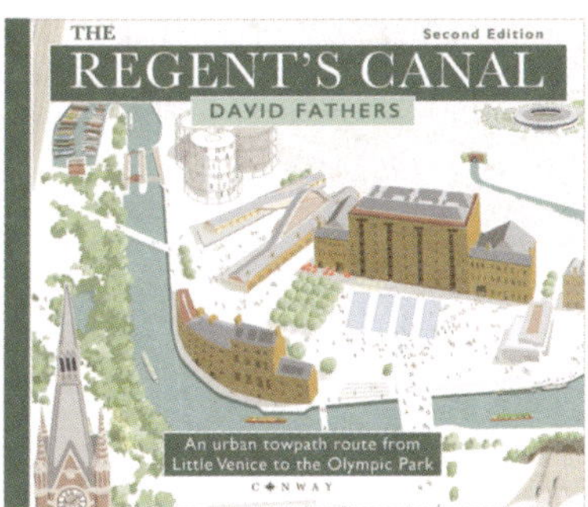

The Regent's Canal (2023)

The London Thames Path (2022)

London's Hidden Rivers (2017)

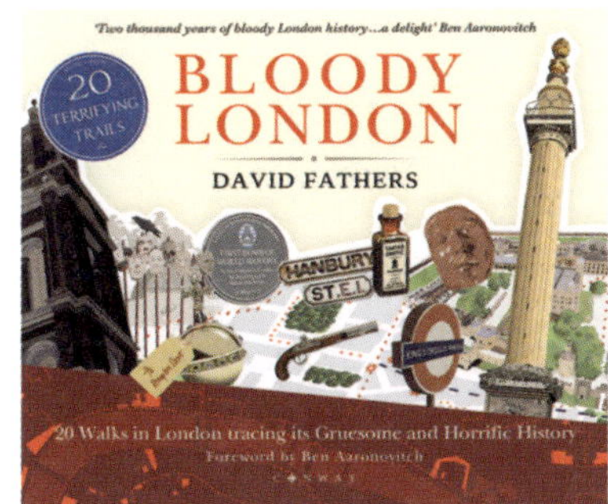

Bloody London (2020)

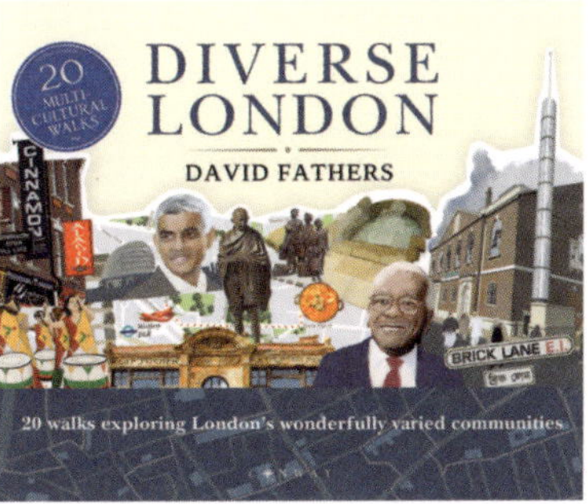

Diverse London (2022)

CONWAY
Bloomsbury Publishing Plc
50 Bedford Square, London, WC1B 3DP, UK
29 Earlsfort Terrace, Dublin 2, Ireland

BLOOMSBURY, CONWAY and the Conway logo are trademarks of Bloomsbury Publishing Plc

First published 2025

Text and illustrations copyright © David Fathers, 2025

David Fathers has asserted his right under the Copyright, Designs and Patents Act, 1988, to be identified as Author of this work

For legal purposes the Acknowledgements on page 150 constitute an extension of this copyright page

A catalogue record for this book is available from the British Library

ISBN: PB: 978-1-8448-6614-4; ePub: 978-1-8448-6613-7; ePDF: 978-1-8448-6612-0

2 4 6 8 10 9 7 5 3 1

Typeset in 8 on 10.2pt Gill Sans Light by David Fathers
Printed and bound in India by Replika Press Pvt. Ltd.

To find out more about our authors and books visit www.bloomsbury.com and sign up for our newsletters